IN AND OUT OF CARE

Child Care Policy and Practice Series
General Editor: Tony Hall
Director and Secretary
British Agencies for Adoption and Fostering

IN AND OUT OF CARE
The experiences of children, parents and social workers

MIKE FISHER
PETER MARSH
DAVID PHILLIPS
with ERIC SAINSBURY

B.T. Batsford Ltd · *London*

in association with

British Agencies for Adoption and Fostering

To our children, Conor, Eimer, Nicholas, Ruth, Alison and Sarah.

© Mike Fisher, Peter Marsh, David Phillips, Eric Sainsbury 1986

First published 1986
All rights reserved. No part of this publication may be reproduced, in any form or by any means, without permission from the Publisher
Typeset by Progress Filmsetting Ltd
and printed in Great Britain by
Billings Ltd, Worcester
Published by B.T. Batsford Ltd
4 Fitzhardinge Street, London W1H 0AH

British Library Cataloguing in Publication Data
Fisher, Mike
    In and out of care: the experiences of children, parents and social
    workers.——(Child care policy and practice)
    I. Child welfare——Great Britain
    1. Title
    2. Marsh, Peter
    3. Philips, David '1949'
    362.7'32'0941   H.V. 751.A6

ISBN 0 7134 5340 0

CONTENTS

ACKNOWLEDGEMENTS

We owe a major debt of thanks to the Economic and Social Research Council for financing this study, and to the Sheffield Family and Community Services Department (social services) for allowing us to undertake it. Many social workers, residential workers, foster parents and clients generously gave us their time and we are very grateful to them for their participation.

The research team was particularly lucky to have the constructive advice and the intelligent criticism of Tony Bottoms, Nick Miller and Marian Barnes. Vicky Simpson, our local research group, and our ESRC 'Northern' group of colleagues provided helpful comments and unflagging support. We greatly valued the links that we had with the Dartington Research Unit and other researchers up and down the country, and we were fortunate in having the unobtrusive administration of Frank Loughran for the ESRC Children in Care Programme. Our secretaries, Christine, Gill, Val and Sylvia, word-processed us into order. The research interviewers, Sue Thompson, Jane Kane, Lynda Ellis and Jackie Ruddock, worked with dedication and skill to provide over 6,500 transcript pages of interviews. Jill Sargeant, our research secretary, coped with us all admirably, even at page 6,499.

1

Introduction

There can be few issues in our society guaranteed to provoke a fiercer debate than the proper care of children. We are all armchair pundits and have all suffered or profited through someone else's child care advice. Curiously, however, this enthusiasm is matched by an almost perfectly counterbalanced reluctance to interfere. The goings-on of the family next door are surrounded by an unchallengeable aura of privacy, within which much child-rearing goes on in virtual secrecy as to its rules and its effects.

This book is about families where that aversion to interfering has been set aside in the interests of the welfare of the children, where private family difficulties have become a matter for public concern. The families we shall tell you about in subsequent chapters have all experienced difficulties in the rearing of their children to such a degree that either they or someone else decided it was necessary to have their children cared for by a public agency – the social services department. Children, parents, residential workers, foster parents and social workers all contributed their accounts. This is the story of how those families found themselves to be in need of help, and what it was like to receive and give that help.

The views and experiences reported here come from those involved in a sample of *all* child care cases with children aged eight and above arising in one social services department over a one year period. These children came into care via the courts and via parental request in all manner of circumstances. They reflect the full range of child care work within this age range encountered in England and Wales. As such, these are not for the most part families in which gross abuse of children has occurred. Indeed, a particular feature of the families we shall encounter is that their difficulties appear very ordinary – a demanding child with behavioural disturbance, an isolated mother with demands exceeding her resources, parental relationships in collision, or teenage children getting into 'trouble'. These are the sorts of difficulties which brought the families we studied to the attention of public agencies. So ordinary were these difficulties that it was a characteristic feature of the social worker's initial response to question their seriousness; after all, most families have these sorts of difficulties to some degree and much stress is concealed behind the wall of privacy. As we shall see (Chapter Three), this apparent ordinariness in fact concealed a chronic erosion of parental tolerance and ability to the point where the question of transgression of privacy became irrelevant.

These families do share something, however, with families where significant abuse has been revealed, and that is the subjection to grossly polarized accounts as to how supposedly normal parents could have come to harm or neglect or fail to control their children. The summer during which this book was finished (1985) was characterized by a long series of child abuse trials, during which parents who seriously assaulted children, or underfed and imprisoned them, or went out leaving them unprotected were described in daily newspapers as 'animals' and as 'killers'. This portrayal of these parents as markedly different from any other parents serves to place their behaviour at a comforting distance, anaesthetizing the raw nerves of every parent who has ever felt extreme anger or incompetence in the face of children's demands. This argument can easily be extended to include all parents of children in care, branding them all as irresponsible and different from the rest of us.

This is the sort of polarized argument often applied to the run-of-the-mill family cases which form the subject of this book. The ring of privacy surrounding families and the reluctance to interfere are such strong influences that any family whose business is opened to public scrutiny becomes by definition different. Once their business is public, however, we are all so well equipped to see what went wrong that our superiority is instantly reinforced. We all 'know' about problem families whose children have to go into care, and we all have images of the homes and the care the children receive. Such families are themselves the subject of official speculation as to the unique qualities which set them apart from other families. Keith Joseph, then Social Services Minister, was able to propose in 1973 that such families possessed in-built characteristics which caused their problems and their continuing use of public welfare through several generations: thus was commissioned a series of studies investigating the theory of 'transmitted deprivation'.

The official sanction given to the notion that families in chronic difficulties were somehow different and deficient forms an important political backdrop to welfare intervention, which is discussed in greater detail in Chapter Seven. What is crucially relevant to the present argument is that this 'knowledge' reinforces public care as the polar opposite of private care within the family, as though the former were exclusively bad and the latter exclusively good. The arguments are conducted in simple terms in order to appeal to simple, supposedly shared values, which in turn will lead to clear verdicts about proper parenting.

Our research began with an open brief to examine the experience of families and workers. We adopted a deliberately naive approach and asked people to tell us their story in their own words. As our picture of care was assembled, we returned to our sources and discussed our understanding of events with them. The accuracy of the unfolding picture was checked and re-checked. Research of this kind inevitably challenges ideological prescriptions for welfare. It makes public the complex world which is so conveniently private and simple for those with an axe to grind.

For example, if many of the difficulties reported by families as leading to admission to care are so ordinary, can it be realistic to propose that these families are fundamentally different in their child-rearing? As we shall see, the difficulties appear from accounts given in this report to be the sort that most parents and most children could overcome, *given sufficient support and guidance*. What sets these families apart from others where similar difficulties arise and are resolved without public help is that they do not have recourse to appropriate support and guidance, rather than that they are constitutionally predestined to disintegration. It follows therefore that, rather than seeking internal family causes, waiting for destiny to assert itself and arranging public child care services to pick up the pieces from a disintegrating family, public policy would be better organized around the principle of giving unstigmatizing support and guidance to families lacking these resources. Included as part of the package of help should be the provision of short periods of care away from the family, such as many middle-class families are able to arrange with relatives and others at particularly demanding times. Because our research reports the experiences of workers alongside those of clients, we pay particular attention to charting the potential opportunities and difficulties in providing this different kind of help.

Help such as this we have termed *assisted parenting*, and in Chapter Eight we describe in detail how this concept might be developed in practice. At this stage, we would simply emphasize the value of such a concept in terms of undermining the antipathy between the care of children within the family and by a public agency. The more possible it is to regard public care as supplementing rather than being a substitute for private care within families, the less distance is allowed to grow between ordinary families and those where a public agency needs to take a hand in parenting.

While research-based work can do much to counter the legacy within child care policy of the polarization of public and private care, it can only do so on certain conditions. We would argue that one of these conditions is that the voices of the clients themselves should be strongly heard within the research findings. There is a direct parallel here with the philosophies underlying family policy. Much social research is carried out according to scientific canons which devalue the subjective element of such areas as clients' perceptions; similarly much family policy regards the families themselves as the passive recipients of welfare, rather than as active participants with cogent views which might change policy. We will argue in Chapters Seven and Eight that in organizing services for families with child care difficulties, both policy and practice must be founded on the principle of *partnership*, in which it is recognized as necessary and valuable to understand the views of clients receiving the service.

In this sense, our research practice of seeking accounts from clients *because the process of welfare intervention cannot be adequately understood without their views* represents for us a paradigm both for understanding and improving the services available to families in need.

In our view, many of the current issues in child care practice would benefit from being re-evaluated in the light of the principle of partnership. For example, a great deal of information has been collected during the past five years on problems in planning for children in care. An initial reason for this work was the apparent drift of children in care without adequate planning, resulting in children needlessly suffering loss of contact with parents or waiting needlessly long periods before substitute parenting was arranged. The research has focused on the professional context of social work planning and the reasons for an absence of active decision-making among social workers. Among the findings are that, in the face of difficult decisions, social workers passively allow the passage of time rather than actual planning to determine the outcomes for children, and that formal organizational arrangements within social services can be a handicap to maintaining adequate supervision which would improve the decision-making of front-line workers. In parallel with this research, social services have developed new practices in child care, reinforcing to professional staff the need for adequate recording and regular managerial review.

What is signally lacking from this approach is a fundamental analysis of the role of the client. The approach can easily assume that planning is solely a professional process in which the proper role for the client is unproblematic and unworthy of investigation. We would argue that any attempt to understand social work planning must take serious account of the views of the client, and must analyse their proper role in the planning and delivery of services.

A guide to the book

It is on account of these beliefs that the client's voice forms an integral part of the chapters which follow. Initially, we sketch in Chapter Two the main characteristics of the families we studied, of the careers in care of their children, and outline our approach to gathering and understanding their views and those of their professional helpers. It is important to understand the limitations and the strengths of the sample of families studied, so that the applicability of our findings to the wider child care process may be assessed. For similar reasons, we describe in some detail the methods used in the study. We believe it is important that studies claiming to represent the clients' views are open to methodological assessment and that, because studies of this kind necessarily rely heavily on large amounts of 'soft' data, this places a further responsibility on the researcher to report in as much detail as space allows the methods used. How this material was gathered, checked, analysed and understood should be of concern to readers wishing to examine the value of our findings.

In Chapters Three to Six, we report the substance of our findings about the differing views brought to the processes of care by mothers, fathers, children and field and residential social workers. We initially explore the origins of care through the recollections of clients of the stresses and strains of family life before contact with social services. While the account may give clues to the reasons for admission to care, we stress that it is premature to seek specific causes, and emphasize instead the influence of past patterns of family difficulties on contact with social services.

In Chapter Four, a detailed account is given of the experiences of clients and workers of admission to care. We emphasize how for families admission to care could be seen as a variation in parenting arrangements rather than as a fundamental break, and how far this concept was from the viewpoint adopted by social workers. In Chapter Five, we continue to explore the experiences of clients and workers of being in care, focusing on residential care. A process of disillusionment among parents, and of powerlessness among children is described, in which the distance between expectations and experience grows.

In Chapter Six clients' and workers' experiences of ending care are explored. We describe how the end of care evolves rather than is decided, and how changes in the child's family during care can make the return home an unfamiliar experience.

In Chapters Seven and Eight we examine the relationship between the findings from the study and current child care policy and practice. In these chapters we undertake a searching re-evaluation of some of the fundamental principles· underlying public intervention in the way families care for their children in private. We hope not only to establish some of the basic ground rules which should govern such intervention, but also to translate them into workable practice models which make sense to practitioners and could be introduced into the everyday working world of social services.

Lastly, let us say a word about our choice of language. Unusually, it has been relatively easy to avoid sexist language; the terms children and young people are usefully neutral. It has been less easy, however, to find terms which avoid patronizing the young. In general, we have used the term child or children when writing of those aged twelve years and below; it is for the older age range that we have struggled to find appropriate words. It is perhaps a comment on our society that the term 'teenagers' has an inappropriate, slightly derogatory ring, and that to refer to them as 'children' would certainly cause offence. As a result, we have generally used the terms 'young person' and 'young people' to refer to those aged thirteen years and above. Although such terms have the merit of impeccable accuracy, they are clumsy and still retain a hint of condescension. If the chapters which follow do anything to alter this state of affairs, it will have been effort well spent.

2

The study, the families, and the children

Introduction

In this project we aimed to explore in depth the views and attitudes and the hopes and fears of all the people involved in a child's admission to care, and their subsequent experiences through to discharge. For any one case, then, we could be interviewing mother, father, child, residential social worker (or foster parents) and field social worker, each on up to three occasions. Obviously it would not be possible, using such intensive methods, to study a very large number of cases, and even though we finally conducted 331 interviews, these related to just 55 cases. In order to situate the detailed study in its wider context, we conducted a document survey of the case-notes of all children in care aged eight or over in the population from which the sample was drawn.

Our host social services department, Sheffield Metropolitan Borough Family and Community Services, had a large enough number of children in care for us to base our study in three of its seven divisions (area teams).

This department, with a £44 million expenditure and 4,000 staff (1984) covered a large and varied metropolitan district with inner city, suburban and near-rural areas. It had an area office fieldwork structure, with each office having around four teams of six social workers and covering one-seventh of the city. Fostering services were based in these offices, but residential and day care services were centrally and separately organized. There was little voluntary sector work in child care. The agency was able to provide a range of cases, and of services, that would be found in social services throughout England and Wales. Children that we studied were in residential short-stay assessment units (often called observation and assessment units) and in small units that attempted to develop a family-like atmosphere (often called family group homes). Others were with foster parents recruited generally, or with foster parents especially found for them. They entered care because their parents requested it (voluntary care) or because courts ordered it (remanded in care and on care orders). Some had experience of brief compulsory care for protection and assessment (place of safety orders). In short the full range of placements and of legal routes was covered in our study.

The study population: children in care and their families

The population from which the sample was drawn comprised all the children aged eight or over who were in care during our fieldwork period in the three social services' divisions that we studied. Our purpose was to provide general background information on these 350 children and their families in order to complement the detailed study in Chapters Three to Six of the cases which form the sample. We undertook a census of those children who were in care on 1 October 1981, plus admissions up to the end of 1982. Comparison with summary data produced by Sheffield Social Services shows that the child-care population in these three divisions accurately reflects that of Sheffield as a whole. Therefore our population is a sub-population of all children aged eight or over in care in Sheffield.

Information was gathered on two areas: family structure, and children's care careers. The purpose of this data-gathering exercise was twofold: first, to provide a sampling frame for the interviews and as a yardstick to assess the sample's representativeness; second, to gain a wide range of information on a large number of children in care and their families, in order to enhance our knowledge of their family situations and care careers.

Family structure

Information on the care careers of the children was readily available in the case files, but family details were less accessible. Indeed, information about occupation and household tenure was missing in many case-records, and had to be excluded from further analysis. The most intractable problem, however, concerned family composition. We very quickly found that a large proportion of the children came from families with a complex and impermanent structure, often with a mix of different parent figures for each child. A not-untypical example of a moderately complex structure can be represented diagrammatically in figure 1.

Mr and Mrs X have seven children between them, two of whom are the product of their own marriage, five from previous marriages. There are four children in their household, their two joint children plus one child from each of their previous marriages. Apart from the substantive

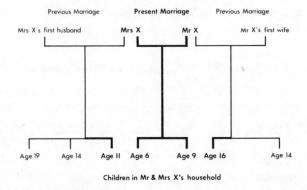

Figure 1. Family structure

issues of child care and role complexity (which are discussed in later chapters), families such as these pose formidable data-coding problems. Unravelling the complexities of family structure also involved a great deal of detective work and detailed scrutiny of case records. In many cases we had to go back to the social workers for elucidation, and in some instances even the social workers did not have full information on the origins of some children. For coding purposes we decided to identify as 'primary parents' those parent figures who were presently, or most recently, associated in a parenting role with each child in the study and parents were then classified as 'natural', 'step' or 'adoptive'.

Incomplete and reconstituted families

The following description – complex though it be – is of necessity a simplification of the labyrinthine nature of family structure which became apparent as the interviews progressed, because it only captures the situation at one point in time. Many families underwent periodic changes of structure with irregular but frequent arrivals and departures of parent figures, sometimes involving the same person in a succession of rifts and reconciliations, sometimes with one person replacing another or transforming a single-parent family into a two-parent family (Rapoport et al, 1982). As will be seen later, these relocations of parent figures often precipitated an admission into care. Nonetheless, the static picture is complex enough, as can be seen from table 1.

It is immediately obvious that only just over one-quarter of the families (27 per cent) are 'normal' two-parent families where both mother and father are natural parents of all children in the household. The remaining three-quarters of the families are either 'incomplete',

9

Table 1 Family structure (% of total families)

	Families without step-children*	Families with at least one step-child	All families
2 parents	27%	21%	48%
1 parent	23%	8%	31%
No parents	7%	2%	9%
Some missing data	8%	4%	12%
Total	65%	35%	100%

No. = 264 families

*i.e if a two-parent family, then both are natural parents to all children; if a single-parent family, then mother or father is a natural parent; if no parents then the last parent figure(s) the child lived with was/were the child's natural parent(s).

'reconstituted', or both (see Burgoyne and Clark, 1982). Just over one-fifth of the families (21 per cent) are reconstituted two-parent families; i.e. families where at least one of the parents is a step-parent to at least one of the children.

There is a prima facie case for supposing that reconstituted families have more than their fair share of problems concerning loyalty, discipline and security. A child with, say, two fathers (a natural father who has remarried and lives outside the household and a 'new' father coming to live with his mother) has to make difficult decisions over loyalty. Similarly, he may resent the new father's attempts to discipline him; or, indeed, his new father may be diffident about attempting to exercise control. In addition, the reality of family reconstitution may have destabilized, or opened the possibility of destabilizing, family ties. We shall have more to say about this issue in later chapters.

It is likely also that greater than average problems of discipline exist in the nearly one-third of families (31 per cent) headed by a single parent (see Chapter Three below). Five-sixths of these are lone mothers. The reconstituted incomplete families (eight per cent of all families) are in a doubly difficult situation in that the single parent is also a step-parent or has children who are step-siblings. Again, five-sixths of these parents are women. In addition, single-parent families headed by a woman are very likely to experience profound financial and housing difficulties (Finer Report, 1974; Streather and Weir, 1974). Most of the 12 per cent of families categorized as having missing data are likely to fall into the single-parent category. Information on the father was unavailable for all but one of these 32 families, and in two-thirds of them it was known that the mother was living in the child's household.

The final nine per cent of families – those with no parents – fall into three categories: first where children are brought up by relatives (usually grandparents or aunts) who have been designated foster parents by the local authority (known in Sheffield as 'de facto fostering'); secondly, children in care from a very early age who have not been adopted, and thirdly those children whose parents have recently died or deserted them, thus precipitating admission to care.

The average number of children per family was 3.5. Nearly half of the families had four or more dependent children. Of the 230 families with more than one child, nearly one-third (31 per cent) had more than one child in care at the time of the survey (21 per cent with two children in care, seven per cent with three, and three per cent with four or more). In addition, information gleaned from the interviews leads us to believe that an additional substantial proportion of siblings had previously been in care.

THE CHILDREN IN CARE

There were 350 children aged eight and over in care in the three divisions. Table 2 shows their distribution by age and sex. It can be seen that the largest single group comprises boys aged 15 or more, with the older girls being the second largest group. In both cases the majority of the children were in the 15 to 16 age group (only 9 per cent of all children were aged over 16). The 15–plus age range was also heavily represented amongst the children recently admitted (41 per cent). These two features lead to the conclusion that a majority of children in the older age group had not been in care for a very long period, and that many of them would be discharged from care before they reached the age of 18.

Table 2 Age by sex (% of all children)

	Boys	Girls	All
8–10 years	8%	9%	17%
11–12 years	11%	4%	15%
13–14 years	11%	12%	23%
15 or older	27%	18%	45%
All	57%	43%	100%

No. = 350 children

One other notable factor is that, while a slightly higher proportion of the youngest children are girls, 11 to 12 year old girls comprise only a very small percentage of the population.

Legal status on admission

Over half the children underwent a voluntary admission into care (62 per cent), one-fifth were admitted under a care order, and around one-tenth each under remand and under place of safety orders. The distribution of legal status categories amongst those of the children recently admitted to care was remarkably similar to that of the whole population.

In relation to age, the percentage of voluntary admissions declined as children grew older, whereas remand and care orders increased. Similarly a higher proportion of girls than boys were admitted voluntarily and the opposite is true for remand and care orders. The relationship between broad age range and sex with legal status on admission is examined in table 3.

Table 3   Legal status on admission by age and sex (% of each age/sex group)

| Sex/age | Legal status | | | | | |
	Voluntary	Place of safety	Remand	Care order	All	No.
Boys under 13	64%	20%	5%	11%	100%	64
Boys over 13	52%	3%	15%	30%	100%	133
Girls under 13	69%	22%		9%	100%	44
Girls over 13	71%	11%	4%	15%	100%	99
Total population	62%	11%	8%	19%	100%	340*

*Information was missing on the legal status on admission of ten of the 350 children. They had all been in care for a considerable period. They were excluded from subsequent analysis.

Several different patterns emerge from this table (see figure 2). The first is that the relative proportions of voluntary admissions are related first to sex, and secondly to age; 70 per cent of female admissions are voluntary compared with 56 per cent of the males. Girls are most likely to be admitted voluntarily, followed by younger boys, then older boys. The same principle applies to remand, but it works in the opposite direction: in other words, older boys are more likely to be remanded than younger boys, who in turn are more likely to be remanded than older girls.

With place of safety orders age is by far the most important factor,

Admission status	MOST LIKELY	LEAST LIKELY
voluntary	FEMALE (younger)	MALE (older)
remanded in care	MALE (older)	FEMALE (younger)
place of safety	YOUNGER (female)	OLDER (male)
care order	OLDER (male)	YOUNGER (female)

Figure 2. Most likely and least likely age/sex characteristics of different legal status on admission. (Secondary characteristics in parenthesis).

mediated by sex; 28 per cent of all under elevens were admitted under a place of safety order, compared with only 6 per cent of the 15–plus age group. A marginally larger proportion of younger girls than boys were admitted compared with a considerably smaller proportion of older boys than girls.

Age is also the most important factor with regard to care orders. Both young girls and young boys have low admission percentages in this category (nine per cent and 11 per cent); older girls are more likely to be admitted under a care order (15 per cent), and older boys are even more likely (30 per cent). But with regard to both remands and care orders the older boys have far higher frequencies of admission than the other groups, as can be seen from figure 2.

Placement on admission

To a very large extent a child's placement when admitted to care is mediated by the legal route of entry he or she has taken, as can be seen from table 4.

Altogether, initial placements on admission fall into three roughly equal groups: fostering, family group home, and reception facilities (including observation and assessment units and community homes with education). But each legal route of entry has its own distinctive placement pattern. Children on remand orders almost always found themselves placed in reception facilities (96 per cent) and none were fostered. Similarly nearly two-thirds of care order admissions were to reception facilities, just one-quarter were to family group homes and only six per cent were fostered.

The majority of voluntary admissions were placed in foster homes (46 per cent) or family group homes (35 per cent) with most of the

13

Table 4 Legal status and placement on admission to care (% of each legal category)

Legal status	Fostered	Family group home	Placement O & A reception or CHE	Other	All	No.
Voluntary	46%	35%	18%	1%	100%	207
Place of safety	21%	40%	21%	18%	100%	38
Remand		4%	96%		100%	27
Care order	6%	28%	63%	3%	100%	68
Total population	32%	32%	33%	3%	100%	340

remainder going to reception facilities (18 per cent). The largest single group of place of safety admissions (40 per cent) were to family group homes, but a wide range of other facilities were also used.

Much of the relationship between age and placement on admission (see figure 2 above), can be explained by legal status. However, with the voluntary admission group there is a relationship between placement and age, with younger children standing a high chance of being fostered and older children being more likely to be admitted to a family group home. This is due to agency policy, where there is an expectation that younger children will be fostered.

Many of the children placed in foster homes on admission will have been admitted some years ago when they were below eight years of age. A smaller proportion of recent admissions will have been placed with foster parents, because of the eight year age threshold of our study. Therefore the figures for the population as a whole do not accurately represent current placement patterns on admission, rather they are an expression of cumulative patterns over a period of a few years (the average length of stay in the population is four and a half years).

CARE CAREERS

Placement changes

One half of the children stayed in their initial placement. This ranged from 74 per cent of children admitted voluntarily down to only 37 per cent of care order children. Many children are admitted to care in the full expectation that they will move on to a second placement (e.g. some place of safety cases; children admitted to a reception home). Table 5 therefore, aggregates the first two placements.

Table 5 Number of placements by legal status on admission (% of each legal category)

Legal status	Number of placements					
	1 or 2	3 or 4	5 or 6	7 or more	All	No.
Voluntary	74%	18%	7%	1%	100%	207
Place of safety	71%	16%	8%	5%	100%	38
Remand	60%	18%	11%	11%	100%	27
Care order	58%	26%	10%	6%	100%	68
Total population	69%	19%	8%	4%	100%	340

A smaller percentage of care order and remand children had two or fewer placements than children admitted through other legal routes. In addition, there is a very strong relationship between length of time in care and number of placements. The average length of time in care for children having one or two placements was four years 20 weeks; three or four placements five years 36 weeks, and for five or more placements seven years 12 weeks, so it is quite likely that number of placements is more strongly associated with length of time in care than legal status on admission.

Placement pathways and destinations

Some types of placements are intended to be more permanent than others, and the care careers of some children are planned as a progression via different placements through to discharge (e.g. reception, family group home, home on trial, discharge). Table 6 shows the percentage of children staying in the same placement, or in the same type of placement during their care career.

The most permanent placements were those known locally as 'de facto fostering' where children had been placed with relatives by their parents, and the social services department formally approved the relatives as foster parents in order to provide them with financial assistance and to monitor the children's progress. These post hoc administrative procedures often formalized long-term and stable child-rearing practices independently negotiated within extended families. This group of cases is then somewhat anomalous. This study only had a small number of such placements in its population, but the

Table 6 Children whose present placement is the same (or of the same type) as their initial placement (as % of initial placements)

Present placement	De facto fostering	Other fostering	Family group home	O & A reception	Other	All
Same placement	100%	53%	63%	38%	14%	50%
Different placement in same placement category		30%	22%	14%		21%
Total in same category	100%	83%	85%	52%	14%	71%
No.	10	99	107	114	10	340

relative stability of the placements has also been shown in the much larger study by Rowe et al (1984).

The permanency levels of the more conventional fostering placements are somewhat disappointing, being only marginally higher than the average for all initial placements (53 per cent compared with 50 per cent). A further 30 per cent of these children stayed within the fostering category but changed foster parents. A small proportion moved from fostering to family group homes (seven per cent) and a further six per cent of children returned home on trial.

A higher proportion of children admitted into family group homes stayed in the same placement (63 per cent) and a further 22 per cent moved to a different family group home (FGH), giving a total staying in the same placement sector of 85 per cent (marginally higher than the fostering total). Very few children moved from FGH to fostering (six per cent) or home on trial (five per cent). Therefore FGHs were the most permanent of the conventional placements. There is no evidence from the data to suggest that any but a small minority of children admitted to FGHs have a planned placement career involving transition to other placement categories.

Placements in reception or observation and assessment centres, on the other hand, are normally intended to be transitional. Less than 40 per cent of children in this category stayed in their initial placement. Over a quarter (26 per cent) were subsequently placed home on trial (often after a transitional stay in a FGH). Around one-eighth transferred to a FGH, possibly progressing along the same route as many who went home on trial. Most of the remainder of the reception group (seven per cent) transferred into foster care (most of these children being in the younger age group).

Previous care episodes

All of the discussion up to this point concerns the current admission of each child. But 30 per cent of the population had been admitted and discharged from care at least once previously, and for 13 per cent of children the current admission was at least the third care episode in their lives. Thus, for a substantial proportion of the children care was not a once-only event, and, in all likelihood, many of the children for whom this was their first care episode would be re-admitted to care later. Girls were more likely than boys to have been in care before (35 per cent compared with 27 per cent), and showed a much greater likelihood of having been in care on more than two occasions (27 per cent compared with nine per cent). When these factors are taken into consideration, along with the fact that girls on average had longer lengths of stay than boys in their present admission, it becomes clear that – in this population – once initially admitted to care, girls were prone to more and longer periods in care than boys.

The relationship between legal status on admission and number of previous care episodes is much more indistinct. A similar proportion of voluntary, remanded and care order children only had one care episode (69 per cent, 67 per cent and 71 per cent respectively). The proportion was higher for children admitted under a place of safety order (78 per cent).

PATTERNS IN CARE

Much has been written about different routes of entry to care and the particular circumstances surrounding criminal proceedings against children. It is the purpose of this section to draw together the strands of children's care careers discussed above, in the hope of identifying patterns in care which can form a framework for discussion in following chapters.

Family structure and legal route of entry into care

It was seen above that only 27 per cent of the families in the population conformed to the stereotype of the 'natural family' of a number of children living with both of their natural parents. Table 7 explores the distribution of natural families within each legal admission status.

Table 7 'Natural families'* by legal status of child on admission (% of each legal status)

| | | Legal status | | | |
	Voluntary	Place of safety	Remand	Care order	All
'Natural families'	18%	29%	41%	33%	24%
All other families	82%	71%	59%	67%	76%
No.	208	38	27	68	341

*'Natural family' = one or more children and both their natural parents sharing the same household.

First of all it can be seen that a smaller number of *children* (24 per cent) than *families* (27 per cent) fitted the natural family category. This is because families with step-siblings have a larger average number of children in care per family than natural families. Voluntary admissions have the lowest proportion of children from natural families (18 per cent) followed by place of safety admissions (29 per cent), care orders (33 per cent) and remands (41 per cent). Even though the proportion of remand children coming from natural families is double that of voluntary admissions, in none of the categories do as many as half of the admissions come from natural families.

Legal entry into care, placement on admission and age-sex distribution

A consistent pattern emerges with regard to these variables, which is not dissimilar to the relationship between legal status and family background. Taken together, place of safety and voluntary admissions exhibit one cluster of attributes directly opposed to the attributes of children remanded into care, with care order admissions between them but closer to remand than voluntary admissions.

Remand: boys, especially older boys from two-parent natural families are most likely to fall into this group, followed by older girls. The overwhelming majority of these children are placed in reception homes.

Care orders: older children rather than younger children, boys more often than girls, from two-parent families are typical of this group.

Reception facilities and FGHs are the most likely placements.

Voluntary and place of safety: these are most likely to be children from incomplete or reconstituted families, girls rather than boys, younger rather than older. They are the most likely to be fostered and the least likely to be admitted to reception homes.

These patterns raise several interesting questions. Are legal categories on admission largely determined by *actions* – either the child's (e.g. offences, truancy) or the parents' (neglect, abuse, exploitation) or by *status* – age, sex of child, family structure? If, as is most likely, there is an interplay between these factors, were there strikingly different patterns of family relationships and child-rearing practices between different legal categories (for example, on the one hand the sudden crisis of arrest and court appearance leading to a care order punctuating an otherwise unexceptional family life, versus on the other hand a gradual accumulation of family problems culminating in voluntary admission)? Or were there remarkable similarities (increasing lack of control, parents reaching the end of their tether, children going off the rails)? It is these, and other similar issues, which the in-depth, sample-based research was designed to explore.

THE IN-DEPTH STUDY

The case-record survey produced much useful information and raised interesting questions. But it was only a backdrop for the main study which aimed to understand the meanings lying behind the information gathered and to try to start answering some of the questions raised.

The primary goal in this research was to gain *understanding* rather than information. We wanted to obtain a clear picture of the feelings, aspirations, hopes and fears of everyone involved in care processes: parents, children, social workers and other helpers. This we hoped would be of direct use to practitioners in their development of 'personal practice models' (Mullen, 1978 and 1983), and in identifying new directions that could be taken to assist clients. In fact, the outcome of the study also has major implications for social work policy makers at both national and local levels.

Research designed to enhance understanding has greater credibility problems than research which provides information. Facts gathered for information purposes can normally be taken at face value. Unless there are major errors in data collection and presentation or – in very rare instances – deliberate falsification of results, we know that different researchers asking the same questions to the same audiences should get broadly similar replies. Furthermore, if samples are properly constructed, statistical tests can be used to assess the applicability of results to the overall population from which the samples are drawn. Thus quantitative surveys can provide hard data which can then be processed, again using increasingly sophisticated procedures, to draw inferences and test hypotheses (for a general discussion of these issues see Reid and Smith, 1981). Throughout these procedures the raw data-set is in principle publicly available. A reader who questions the validity of a survey's results can carry out checks by using the original questionnaire returns.

Research aimed at enhancing understanding, however, is of a very different nature. The most important difference is that the facts to be collected are less tangible than those used for most information purposes. 'Facts for information' are those which generally fulfil the dictionary definition of 'things certainly known to have occurred or to be true' (e.g. the legal status of a child's admission to care, or the number of previous admissions). A 'fact for understanding' on the other hand is normally a 'datum of experience' where 'datum' is defined as 'an assumption or premise from which inferences may be drawn' (Concise Oxford Dictionary).

Therefore even if research aimed at increasing understanding uses the same statistical *methods* as information-research, its raw material is softer and more elusive. For example even the most sophisticated and reliable attitudinal or personality scales purport to measure attributes which are, at best, extremely complex and resistant to clarification. Most understanding-research moreover does not use these statistical and quantitative techniques, partly because the research material is often not amenable to this type of analysis, and partly because the research results are usually better expressed in qualitative rather than quantitative form. It is the *methods* of qualitative research analysis which give the most cause for concern. In some research reports there appears to be a disparity between the conclusions drawn and the small amount of evidence provided (usually in the form of snippets of interview transcripts) and in others the conclusions are presented without supporting evidence, leaving the reader in limbo. Often too, qualitative research reports give the appearance of self-fulfilling prophecies, containing findings entirely consonant with the author's previously known ideological or theoretical stances (for discussion of this issue see Phillips, 1983).

Analysing soft data is extraordinarily difficult. For a start there is always so much of it, and there are none of the statistical short cuts which are available for quantitative material. Nevertheless it is possible to analyse soft data just as rigorously as hard data, and the results of qualitative research, although they can seldom be stated precisely in numeric form, can be demonstrated to be as reliable and valid as the results of quantitative research.

There are several important issues which need to be resolved before the accuracy and credibility of qualitative research can be justified.

The first concerns *data collection*. To be of use the data must be free of bias, and it needs to be reliable in reflecting what was said, and valid in representing what was meant, by respondents. Also it needs to be available to other researchers for scrutiny. Secondly the *sample* selected must be comparable in a meaningful way with the population from which it was drawn, and any unavoidable sampling biases need to be identified and taken into account when presenting findings. Thirdly *data analysis* must be rigorous and tested for bias and errors of inference. Also, ideally it should be tested for meaningfulness in relation to the raw data: this would normally involve presenting research participants with interim findings and ascertaining whether it 'rang true' to them. Finally the analysis of data from the sample must be related to the wider population.

The research project

A brief summary of the structure of the research is necessary before outlining the ways that this study approached the issues of reliability and validity. Our major interest concerned the perceptions and subjective experiences of care as seen by the service users, social workers and other professionals at various stages in children's care careers. In order to achieve this we decided to follow some children through their care careers, interviewing them, their families and helpers at the following stages: on admission, whilst in care and, if possible, upon discharge. These longitudinal cases would provide the backbone of the research project. Because fieldwork could last for only 12 months, however, it was unlikely that many children could be completely followed through in this manner. Therefore it would be possible to interview many of the cases on one occasion only. These 'snapshot' cases would be used to augment information gained from longitudinal cases and would provide a breadth of information and analysis.

The target group of children was aged eight years and upwards. Given the centrality of the child's views, we wished to maximize our chances of obtaining the highest possible quality of data from the children themselves. Therefore we decided to avoid interviewing children under eight. We proposed to sample roughly equal proportions of boys and girls and to ensure that the whole of our age range was represented. Similarly we wished to achieve a spread of admission categories in the first phase of the study, and to cover all the most important types of placement in the 'in-care' phase.

Our original intention was to follow 40 children through admission, interview them again whilst in care, and interview a third time the 20 or so of them whom we expected to leave care during the year. An additional 20 snapshot cases would be interviewed for the first time on discharge. We also intended to follow up ten longitudinal and ten snapshot cases after discharge. Thus we wished to interview the relevant participants in 60 cases, giving 140 sets of interviews (40 in each of the first three phases and 20 in phase four) with an average of four to five interviews per set.

DATA COLLECTION

The issue of bias

Our primary concern throughout the research project was to ascertain as accurately as possible the experiences and perceptions of the people involved in care over a period of time. This had to be done in a way which enabled them to identify the issues which *they* considered to be important. Therefore at the beginning of each interview individual participants were asked to narrate the story of previous events and to give an account of their opinions and attitudes. At the end of the narration the interviewer asked for a summary of the most important factors. Specific questions were then asked about the current situation and about that individual's views of the other people involved. Care was taken to ensure that these specific questions did not 'put words into their mouths' (see Phillips, 1983).

This combination of open-ended, respondent-led narration, and non-leading, specific questions, overcomes most of the problems of research design bias. The narratives dispose of negative bias (i.e. excluding or undervaluing important issues); indeed, many important issues, of which we had been previously unaware, emerged from the narratives. These would not have come to light if we had relied solely upon structured interviewing techniques. The dangers of positive bias (i.e. including or overvaluing unimportant, or even non-existent issues) were reduced by careful presentation of specifically aimed questions. In order to be as cautious as possible about bias we imposed a further check by noting whether these areas had previously emerged from the narrations.

An interesting example of this process can be seen in relation to questions we asked about legal status on admission. There has been discussion in the literature about parents' concerns regarding their children's legal status (e.g. Parker, 1980). We found from the social worker interviews in the first phase of the research that great care had been taken to keep parents fully informed and to allay any fears they might have. Yet much to our surprise both parents and children seemed peculiarly uninterested in this subject. On checking with the narratives we found little mention of it. So in the second phase of the research we explored the issue more deeply and found a strong preoccupation with a somewhat different issue; that of *moral* rather than legal sanction. The substance of this issue is explored in Chapter Four, but its importance for methodology is best summarized here. First, if the research had comprised one-off interviews with no narrative but with a pre-coded question on legal status we would have obtained biased and misleading results. Secondly, if the research had comprised one-off interviews with a narrative and pre-coded legal status question, we would have been able to identify the problem but could not have resolved it. It was the *combination* of multi-phase interviewing, specific but non-precoded questions and a respondent-led narrative, which minimized rather than merely reduced the danger of positive bias. As can be seen below we took further steps to avoid the danger of interviewer bias as well as research design bias.

Reliability and validity

The issues of reliability and validity loomed very large in our discussions of research design. With regard to our data, we took considerable pains to ensure reliability. Standard procedures of asking similar questions in different ways at different points within interviews fitted well to our interview process, which entailed approaching the same themes from different perspectives, using a variety of interviewing techniques. In addition, reliability checks were undertaken in the longitudinal cases between interviews where some of the recapitulative questions specifically probed reliability issues. In addition we were able to check for consistency between narratives across the phases in these cases.

Problems concerning the validity of the data were of a rather different order. Given that our concern was with people's perceptions rather than with 'hard facts' we did not have to decide which of two participants' views on the same issue was 'right' and which was 'wrong' – only on whether we had understood their perceptions correctly. For example, if a mother said she believed that the social worker was genuinely concerned about her child's welfare whereas the father said he thought the social worker was indifferent on this issue, so long as we had no reason to doubt their truthfulness or to believe that they had misunderstood the questions, then both replies were considered to be valid representations of the individuals' views.

We were initially concerned about this issue of truthfulness. It is well known, for example, that prisons are full of people fervently proclaiming their innocence (not all of whom are being entirely honest), and we expected that many families whose children had been admitted to care for committing offences would 'launder' their accounts to minimize familial blame. Contrary to our expectations, we found no reticence amongst respondents in disclosing personally unpalatable factors to interviewers. Thus we had no reason to believe that respondents were being consistently dishonest in those areas where one would most expect it.

A more difficult issue relates to the possibility of respondents constructing with the benefit of hindsight a post hoc rationalisation of previous events, perceptions and feelings, which does not tally with what happened at the time. This problem becomes particularly difficult where, for example, respondents are asked about their perceptions of another participant's actions over a period of time. One issue which highlights this problem is that defined later as 'fatalistic-resignation' where we found that virtually all mothers expressed a fatalistic attitude about the child's admission to care. It is very difficult to assess whether or not this view has been restructured with hindsight by the participants. The most that can be hoped for in this area is that we faithfully recorded participants' contemporary views about what they had previously thought or felt.

Availability of data

In principle, if all interviews are tape recorded and transcribed, data should be available to other researchers. In practice we soon came to understand why data was not available from previous studies. Tapes are expensive and transcription is a time-consuming process. Many previous researchers have apparently listened to their tapes, taken notes (instead of transcribing), then erased the tapes for reuse in subsequent interviews. Our determination to save all data led to the creation of a library of 331 tapes and 6,500 pages of typed transcript (the equivalent in length of 25 text books). Transcription alone, excluding proof-reading, took over one and half person-years of typing. Availability to other researchers is still difficult, of course, because of the problems of confidentiality.

Sampling

Sampling was undertaken in two stages. First, in order to husband our resources, and to concentrate our efforts on identifying children at the point of entry into care, we undertook the research in the three (out of seven) social services divisions which had the highest number of child-care admissions per year in the eight-plus age range. This inevitably biased the sampling-frame towards those geographical areas in the city with a high incidence of care admission episodes; i.e. densely populated inner-city areas. Nevertheless we found, from comparison with city-wide statistical returns, that the sub-population of care admissions in these divisions was typical of admissions in the city as a whole in terms of demographic and socio-economic factors.

The second stage, identifying and gaining access to cases where a child was being admitted into care, was much more difficult than was initially expected (Phillips and Marsh, 1984). All-in-all we had a 'failure rate' of nearly 50 per cent in gaining access to families and children; 32 per cent refusals (14 per cent parents, 14 per cent social workers and four per cent children) and 14 per cent where access was impossible. Access was impossible either because of delays (often indefinite) imposed by social workers where they believed immediate access was not in the client's best interests (nine per cent), or because we previously had access to two cases belonging to the same social worker. A limit of two cases was imposed in order to avoid skewing the sample and to ensure that no social worker had an unduly large burden as a research respondent.

Case-notes of 'access failures' were scrutinized (as part of the contextual population study) and did not appear to be untypical in socio-demographic or social work practice factors, although there were more voluntary and less statutory admissions than expected. Thus, apart from admission status, we have no evidence that 'lost' *clients* were atypical. The situation was rather different, however, with regard to *social workers*. Access to nearly a quarter of the potential sample had been blocked by social workers. Although this occurred in many cases for good reason, it soon became obvious that a few workers were not prepared to allow access to any of their cases. It is highly likely (indeed we feel sure it is certain) that the social worker sample was somewhat biased, under-representing (possibly wholly omitting) practitioners who were loth to expose their work to research scrutiny. We cannot be sure of the effects of this bias in the sample of social workers, but it is probable that the participating social workers were in general more confident in their practice and more committed to social work research than the non-participants. This factor is mirrored in most other similar studies (e.g. Sainsbury et al, 1982) but it does need to be remembered that the social worker sample is biased.

The major result of the high 'failure rate' in sampling was that we were unable to pick and choose cases in relation to our initial age-sex-status-placement criteria. We had to take almost every case offered. This led to an unavoidable under-representation of voluntary admissions. It is probable that a hidden bias is at work here. Most care order admissions are seen as unavoidable once the precipitating event has taken place. Voluntary admissions, though, are often seen as potentially avoidable, and very often within Sheffield Social Services they appeared to be seen as representing a failure of preventive work. It is possible, therefore, that cases where social workers are dissatisfied with their own work are under-represented owing to a reluctance to expose examples of dissatisfying work. Interestingly, Sainsbury et al (1982) found higher levels of dissatisfaction in voluntary than statutory cases when doing research in the same agency.

One further bias was deliberately created. We decided not to interview in those very rare cases where the parents could not speak English. Apart from this, the differences between the sample and the population can be explained entirely in terms of factors associated with a low incidence of voluntary admissions (i.e. some under-representation of lower age groups and of foster placements). In general the sample was very robust and, taking the above factors into account, was representative of the population as a whole.

In relation to the criteria for sampling discussed earlier: the first criterion, that the sample can be meaningfully compared with the population, was met by scrutinizing all case-notes of children aged eight or more years in care in the three divisions.

We found that the sample was a remarkably robust representation of the population, given that it, of necessity, had an inbuilt emphasis towards recent admissions. Overall, the sex distribution of the sample mirrored that of the population and the age distribution was almost the same, excepting a slight over-representation of 13 to 14 year olds in both sexes (29 per cent compared with 24 per cent) and under-representation of boys less than 11 years old (four per cent rather than eight per cent) noted above. Voluntary cases were under-represented (43 per cent instead of 57 per cent) and remands were heavily over-represented (19 per cent instead of eight per cent); all other statuses were similar. Foster placements were under-represented because of the relative over-concentration on more recent admissions where foster placements were less common than we had expected. The sample was representative on number of placements and on the relationship between the number of placements and legal status on admission. Average length of stay was considerably shorter (three years four weeks compared with five years 32 weeks), because of the emphasis in the sample upon admission cases.

One of the most encouraging things about the sample was that, although of necessity it over-emphasised recent admissions and remands, it fairly and accurately represents the inter-relationships between the relevant attributes in the population which are discussed in the first section of this chapter.

With regard to the second sampling criterion (on bias) the following areas were identified as sources of bias:

(a) Non-English speaking clients were excluded from the study,
(b) Social workers unwilling to participate excluded themselves from the study.
(c) It is possible that voluntary admissions, where social workers felt dissatisfied with their previous work, are under-represented (although some courageous workers did give access to this type of case, openly admitting their dissatisfaction with the outcome).

One other potential area of bias, arising from the interviewers themselves, is discussed later.

The sample

The sample comprised 55 cases, giving rise to 331 individual interviews. In 28 cases respondents were interviewed on one occasion only (12 in the admission phase, seven in the in-care phase, and nine in the discharge phase). In a further 23 cases respondents were interviewed on two occasions (19 in both admission and in-care phases, three in both in-care and discharge phases and one in both admission and discharge phases). Finally, in four cases respondents were interviewed in all three phases. Thus altogether there were 86 'interview sets' (28 'one-phase' sets, 23 × 2 = 46 'two-phase' sets and 4 × 3 = 12 'three-phase' sets). On average there were nearly four interviews per interview set (e.g. mother, child, field social worker, residential social worker). Table 8 identifies the range of interviews per set.

Table 8 Number of interviews per interview set

	1	2	3	4	5	6	All
No. of sets	1	4	28	30	20	3	86
Total no. of interviews	1	8	84	120	100	18	331

It can be seen that the majority of interview sets had three, four or five interviews per case in each phase (although the average number of interviews per set declined between the admission and discharge phases). There were 148 interviews in the admission phase, 129 in the in-care phase, and 54 in the discharge phase.

Table 9 Interviews by respondent

Respondent	No.	%
Mother	61	19
Father	32	10
Child	79	24
Sibling(s)	14	4
Field social worker	80	24
Residential social worker	34	10
Other social worker	8	2
Foster mother	14	4
Foster father	9	3
	331	100

It can be seen that around two-thirds of all interviews were with field social worker, mother and child.

Figure 3 gives an example of a rather complicated situation of a family interviewed in all three phases. The admission phase and in-care phase interview sets each comprised five interviews, and the discharge phase set comprised three interviews.

(For the sake of simplicity, only a skeletal framework is shown – the mother's interview was, of course, analysed in relation to the social worker's, foster mother's and foster father's as well as to the child.)

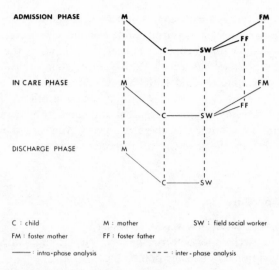

C : child   M : mother   SW : field social worker

FM : foster mother   FF : foster father

————— : intra-phase analysis   — — — — : inter-phase analysis

Figure 3. The Baker family interviews.

DATA ANALYSIS

Analysing these complex interviews was of course a monumental task. An important and profound conclusion we arrived at concerning research methodology was that qualitative research workers need to be blessed with longevity in order to be able to stand a chance of mastering their data.

Before discussing substantive issues of data analysis, it is worth noting some of the steps taken to reduce the problems of interviewer bias. The majority of interviews were undertaken by three part-time research interviewers. Each was a social science graduate with post-graduate academic and professional qualifications (two were qualified social workers, one was an educational psychologist). Before undertaking pilot research interviews they undertook a course of briefing and training sessions which covered the aims and methods of the research study, child care legislation and practice, and data-collecting skills. Particular attention was paid to professional de-socialisation in order that they did not unwittingly associate themselves unduly with the social workers' rather than the clients' perspective. Their pilot interviews were taped and transcribed and these recordings and transcripts were then used as training tools. Also, transcripts in the main study were carefully checked for possible interviewer bias.

Qualitative interviews are much less impersonal than those designed for quantitative purposes and it is impossible to achieve total conformity of interview style. We found that this appeared not to affect the *quality* of data collected, but we suspect that different personal styles may have affected the *quantity* of data gathered. One interviewer consistently achieved longer interviews with children than the others. However, after careful scrutiny of the conceptual and theoretical issues arising from the data it was found that there was a very even spread both in the substance and in the pattern of responses amongst the research interviews.

Analysis procedure

Analysis for each interview was in five stages:

1. The research interviewer taped a brief impressionistic post-interview summary of major points.

2. The research officer read transcripts, noting evolving conceptual categories, gathering evidence in support of or contrary to previously defined categories, and watching for new conceptual or theoretical material. Page-referenced notes, along with quotes, were recorded on index cards. At the same time any ambiguities in responses were noted and a watch was kept for possible interviewer biases. Separate files were kept for these purposes.

3. The research officer discussed the transcripts with the research interviewer, using a research approach towards the interviewer similar to that used by the interviewer towards the interviewee. Any ambiguities or possible biases were discussed. This was followed by a detailed discussion of the conceptual issues identified by the research officer to check with the interviewer's impression. Often this led to replaying critical parts of the tape and annotation of the transcript. this was particularly important with parent interviews where a wry or sometimes ironic sense of humour was often displayed. Meanings which were obvious when listening to tapes were often obscure when reading transcripts.

4. Then the transcripts were read by one or more of the other members of the research team. At this stage, interviews were usually read in interview sets including all interviews for one case in one phase. This enabled the researchers to pick up interconnections between interviews in the same set which might have been missed by the research officer who had to analyse each interview separately as soon as possible in order to be able to liaise effectively with the

research interviewer. This meant he was often unable to analyse interviews from the same set sequentially. Every case which threw up important or particularly clear examples of conceptual or theoretical interest was analysed 'blind' by all researchers.

5. Finally the researchers compared notes. One of the most gratifying aspects of this work was the high level of agreement reached on most major issues. The most striking feature about this process was that very often more than one of the researchers would light upon a completely new issue independently of each other.

As this process continued, several themes started to emerge. When enough evidence was gathered for each one, a working paper was written including extensive quotations from transcripts. Each working paper was presented to a research group comprising social service research officers, residential and field social workers and a team leader. This usually led to lively and critical discussions which often concluded in the paper being modified and the concepts being refined. Also, in many instances, before a finding was finally accepted, it had to go through two more stages: co-research and agency workshops.

The notion of co-research as expressed in this project is, we believe, an important one in qualitative research in the area of the personal social services. Its purpose was to utilize some of the research subjects as research workers in the analysis stage. It was not used to check out their own individual experiences directly but to enable them to assess the verismilitude of our general findings. Methodologically, we found co-research to be extraordinarily useful. In practical terms, however, its major drawback relates to the resources needed and the time lost in organization. For example, the two co-research sessions we held with children were phenomenally difficult to organize, and we had to abandon the sessions with mothers because so few were able to attend.

Briefly, the procedure adopted in the co-research session was firstly to identify important issues, then collect as many relevant quotations as possible, anonymize them and present them unadorned as a basis for a tape-recorded discussion. The following subject areas were covered in eight sessions:

Field social workers and residential social workers: discipline in home and in care, and secondly, parental responsibility.

Field social workers: mothers and fathers as distinct clients, and secondly, social work as mitigation.

Fathers: care as discipline, and secondly, social work as surveillance.

Children: care as an attractive option (two sessions).

Five half-day workshops were held towards the end of the research project, with membership representing a range of workers. The topics covered were:

Parents' rights, responsibilities and the legal framework of care.

Residential work and its relationship to fieldwork.

Social work with families with a teenager beyond their control.

Minimizing damage to clients.

Achieving effective partnership with clients.

Detailed papers were presented to each workshop, and the workshops operated in a similar fashion to the research group. Each workshop's discussion was summarized and the collected summaries were then presented to a senior management meeting.

The complex network of analysis procedures throughout the research process was necessitated by two factors. The first was our decision to employ a qualitative rather than quantitative research design. The issues under study were many-sided and were situated in the subtle interplay of personal relationships. Social work is a *personal* social service which respects the individual uniqueness of the persons who are clients: social work research loses much of the 'truth' in social work practice, unless it too respects the multi-dimensional forces at play in situations where social work takes place.

Secondly, within this qualitative design, we wished to take as many steps as were feasible to ensure accuracy and valid inference. Therefore, throughout data gathering and analysis we utilized iterative and recursive research techniques. In addition, the procedure of 'methodological triangulation' was used in order both to illuminate and cross-check our findings from several different perspectives. These steps were undertaken in order to fulfil the first three acceptability criteria of maximum rigour, a minimum of errors of inference, and minimal bias. The fourth criterion (that of meaningfulness) was met by the co-research and agency workshop sessions. The fifth criterion, the relation of the sample to the population from which it was drawn, was achieved with the case-record survey discussed in the first part of this chapter.

3

Experiences prior to care

Introduction

It is a dangerously misleading question to ask why a child came into care. It is difficult, but necessary, to resist the temptation to resolve the messy world of social reality into an answer, comforting in its precision if not in its content. We are only just beginning to understand the numerous factors we must take singly into account, let alone the multiplicity of ways in which they interact. Nor must we ever forget that the social mechanisms we may wish to highlight as contributing to family disruption are subject to the infinitely variable uniqueness of their human participants.

This chapter concerns, therefore, the antecedents of care in the sense of exploring the stresses and strains of life in the families we studied and the attitudes of family members. It is not primarily about the reasons why the young people we studied entered care – although some answers to this question may suggest themselves from the information presented here – but about the way these families function, the implications of this for their contacts with social services, and about workers' initial reactions to these families.

The stress of parenting

The difficulties over the care of their children which brought families into contact with social services were extremely long-standing. Almost without fail, parents would describe their current difficulties as having started many years ago when the child was much younger.

> Mother: It started a few years ago, after my first husband left. I found money had gone missing, she was about eight at the time . . . She's a child that's never satisfied . . . very sort of strong-minded . . . As she's got older [she had reached 15] the problems have got bigger.

> Mother: He wouldn't go to school. He's been doing it for three, four years, probably longer . . . He used to have nightmares . . . he got done for shoplifting . . . But this schooling still carried on, I've had education authority five or six times, but he never got any different [he had reached 15].

This long-term perspective on the problems parents experienced applied equally to pre-teen children.

> Mother: [of her ten year old daughter] She has terrible behaviour problems, it's the screaming and banging . . . This has been – how long? Since she was six months old really . . .

This sense of the history of family difficulties was an important clue to how parents saw their children. In effect they were seen as responsible for *continuous* stress over periods of at least three or four years and, in some cases, over ten years. Parenting was described as a burden and it was wrong that help had not been offered earlier. No-one 'really knew what it was like' for them to live with a difficult child, and social workers were not very good at recognizing the stress they were experiencing.

> Mother: According to the social services, she wasn't bad enough to be actually taken into care. This I thought was wrong because they only saw her perhaps once every two or three months or when I got on the phone and cried for help . . . We lived with her all the time, we had to suffer with this.

> Mother: I know somebody else who had problems, but they [social services] jumped to them sort of thing when they wanted help . . . When I needed it, when I was really down, and I mean *really* down, that time it's as though nobody wanted to know.

A sense of bitterness and frustration characterized these mothers' accounts of trying to convince others that they needed help. Underlying this was a sense of never having anything good back from their children, a sense of having lost any possibility of gaining pleasure from children – 'I thought, well, I've brought seven kids up and this is what I get, all on my own I fetched them up'. This sense of injustice and of loss, backed up with the burden of years of coping with difficulties, constituted a formidable backdrop to the current crisis, and, as will later be demonstrated, proved a considerable stumbling block in assessing with social workers what was wrong and what should be done about it.

Thus the current crisis had to be seen as one of many, each of which contributed to the gradual erosion of the parents' coping abilities and of their sense of having an active influence over the lives of their children. Parents frequently expressed the view that it was only 'natural' that children should test out the limits, and that parenting a growing child involved a process of instilling control and discipline, possibly using physical sanctions. Three parents:

I think he must have a bit of authority somewhere.

A boy does need a bit of discipline.

She's got to be made to realize, [i.e. that there are limits to what will be tolerated].

A distinct strand emerged around the theme of '*danger on the streets*'. If children were primed to encounter trouble, it was on the streets that it was going to happen. They would be led astray by other, tougher kids and the gang mentality would encourage behaviour which otherwise would not have surfaced. Two children:

Sometimes you can be just walking past and get carried off.

If you follow other kids that are doing things that is wrong, whether you do it or not, so long as you're in that group, you will get into bad trouble.

It was in these circumstances that 'thieving', 'shoplifting' and (for girls) 'going to bed with men' occurred. An image was created of city life where merely being out and about was dangerous, and much parental effort was expended in trying to control the amount of time children were exposed to 'danger on the streets'.

This theme also allowed parents to imply that their own child was different, not like the other kids on the street.

These young lasses, about three or four of them, were on the game. Some were shoplifting, all buddies anyway. So I were quite proud inwardly knowing that my lad didn't go in for anything like that.

Probably these parents, like most others, considered their child uniquely innocent or at least uniquely exculpated by mitigating circumstances where offences were committed in groups. Moreover, the fear that a child might be contaminated by contact with other children liable to be admitted to care was a persistent theme in parents' later attitudes towards care (see Chapter Five).

As they grew older, children's challenges became more powerful and had to be met with a firm hand. This was felt to be an extremely difficult task in a society which frowned on physical sanctions and on too many restrictions on children. Parents felt in a general sense that children nowadays paid less attention to their parents ('When I was her age, I had to ask permission to breathe') and that a punitive approach laid the parents open to the risk of interference from police or from 'the welfare'. At a later stage in the research, parents were asked directly whether they felt their rights over their children were the same now as they used to be when they were themselves children. Over two-thirds of mothers and fathers replied that they felt their rights had decreased as compared with those they ascribed to their parents. There was an overwhelming feeling from these parents of distance between themselves and their children ('Children today are a different class of folk than they were in the fifties and sixties') and constant reference was made to lack of 'respect' and of 'manners'. As the need for discipline increased, parents became less sure how to exercise it effectively. The task of giving discipline was essentially seen as ideally shared between parents, not least because it was described as most effective if it was immediate: it could not, therefore, await the return home of the one parent who meted out punishment. This was, however, very much the ideal. As we shall see, few families in practice had the consistent services of fathers in this task and mothers regretted this bitterly.

He needs that male influence.

His problem is he won't be gaffered.

He needed a male that could dominate to a certain extent.

There were some differences between the parents regarding their views of discipline. This difference revolved around the extent to which *firmness* – on the necessity for which both were agreed – involved physical punishment. Some fathers believed that physical punishment was effective in decreasing disobedience and advocated 'a quick scutch' in preference to other sanctions or just talking. Mothers, on the other hand, tended to talk of the child's need to have 'respect' for adults and to accept their firmness ('He's got to learn there's always someone to tell him what to do'); mothers tended to emphasize the abstract qualities of the relationship they would like to see between their child and the adult world (e.g. 'He needs that male influence') and other sanctions tended to be attempted ahead of physical punishment. This is not to say that these mothers repudiated physical punishment at all, rather its presence as a symbolic ultimate deterrent was underlined as necessary to the demonstration of firmness towards children: indeed mothers sometimes referred to their own lack of credibility in the eyes of the child as a physical force to be reckoned with, as forming a significant handicap to their parenting.

However, as the data presented in Chapter Two demonstrates, fathers were far from a constant figure in the lives of these families. In only one-quarter of the total population of families was the natural father present as well as the mother, and in only around one-half of the families was a father figure present at all. Our interview sample for the initial stage of the research also reflected father absence: for only 39% of the children was the natural father or father figure available for interview. One-third of the children lived in single-parent families headed by the mother.

Research interviews were frequently complicated by the necessity to clarify whether the father being discussed was in fact still living with the family, or whether all children shared the same parents ('The oldest one, she's not his, you see'). The problems that the absence or replacement of fathers bring to families have been extensively explored by sociologists of family life (e.g. Rapoport et al, 1977). Typical of such families is the way in which, in the families we studied, the turnover of father figures reduced their role in the disciplining of children and left mothers to cope on their own. Typical also was the mothers' response that they did not feel that this role came naturally to them.

As they get older, it's harder for a woman to discipline a boy.

My problem is my 'No' isn't 'No'.

They felt it was difficult to persuade the new husband or cohabitee to take on this role since this might expose him to stress and possible rejection by the children, threatening the fragile stability of the family. In any case, if they weren't 'his' then you couldn't really expect 'him' to be responsible for them. So the mothers coped as best they could, feeling ill-equipped for a demanding role and unsupported in this by either husband/cohabitee or wider society.

Not surprisingly, this was described as a desperately discouraging experience. Sons and daughters began to suspect that, if they pushed to the limits, they could get away with behaviour which would formerly have provoked a severe clamp-down from father. Sensing this, mothers sometimes called in uncles to exercise 'that male influence' or tried to make the eldest boy into a responsible figure whose job it was to set standards.

Mother: Big lad, he's nineteen, I used to let him chastise them, let him be man, because I'm divorced, one-parent family, and I used to let him take father's place.

But these were at best only temporary solutions and the strain of parenting began to exact its toll.

Very early on in the research, particularly in interviews with mothers, we had been surprised to encounter a strong sense of *fatalism* in parents' attitudes. While we had been prepared for anger, or attempts to justify themselves to us as parents, we had not expected such a degree of what appeared to be passive acceptance of loss of authority over children and of the intervention of police, the courts and social services. The story of how we became sensitized to this issue and how we attempted to understand it in terms of the clients' world illustrates well our research approach.

Our interview schedule concerning admission to care included several probes about whether clients felt that what had happened was unavoidable (e.g. 'Looking back, do you think things could have happened differently?'). It was in replies to this question that we found much of the evidence for the theme of 'naturally' unruly children, inevitably testing the limits of parental discipline as they grew up. But further strands of evidence concerning attitudes of resignation became apparent in the way some mothers would describe appalling events in a bland, deadpan manner without evidence of distress. In their seeming unconcern and unemotionality about severe family disruptions, these respondents often contradicted the predictions, not to mention warnings, of their social workers to the researchers.

Evidence of this bland unemotionality is obviously difficult to set out in written form, since much of it derives from listening to the tape recording of the interview. It is in any case 'negative' evidence – it is what did *not* happen or what was *not* expressed which is important (for a discussion of the value of 'negative' evidence in social research, see Lewis and Lewis, 1980). However, some events described in the interviews which were unaccompanied by apparent distress may give the flavour of this feeling. In one case, a mother described how her son left home after a dispute to live with a neighbour until she in turn ejected him; in another, the mother seriously proposed that none of this would have happened had she not gone shopping on a particular day; in another, an attack on her daughter by prison officers, resulting in internal damage, was described; a 'revenge' attack on the house, involving the breaking of a window was described; a complete lack of knowledge was expressed about the possible length of time care would last.

As part of our methodological approach, we also asked the research interviewers to record their initial impressions, or 'first-form inferences' (Schwartz and Jacobs, 1979), of the respondents. This information gave important clues to the atmosphere of the interview and further supported the view that these mothers showed attitudes of resignation.

Her other son is to appear in court tomorrow on charges of burglary. She seemed to accept this in the same way [as she accepted child's going into care] as being fate . . .

[On the revenge attack] She expressed no emotion about this at all – just mild acceptance.

I didn't really think Mrs King was forthcoming about everything . . . I think a lot of fatalism came through . . . and maybe this was due to her attitude that it [care] was practically expected to happen.

[On daughter's admission to care and police charges] She didn't resent this at all . . . She didn't question the fact . . . She just took it as the case and accepted it and the outcome of it. There was no sort of emotion there, it was just very matter of fact this is what had happened . . .

It is important to note that comments of this type originated independently from all three researchers who undertook the bulk of the initial interviewing.

It was possible to advance many hypotheses to explain these attitudes in parents, and care was taken to examine a range of possible explanations. Mothers might have simply concealed their distress: yet the interviews contained detailed expositions of extremely intimate aspects of respondents' lives (often more detailed and intimate than was requested), and the researchers reported much frankness, directness and warmth in the interviews. Mothers might have had to tell their tale so frequently to others that they had become desensitized to its impact: yet the researchers frequently reported relief in respondents at the chance to tell their story, rather than staleness, and, in some cases, events under discussion had only just taken place and it was therefore unlikely that respondents had had the time to grow used to their impact. Another possibility was that these mothers were seriously depressed and unable to generate appropriate emotional responses; this was felt to apply to only two of the mothers interviewed and did not in any case account for the element of acceptance in their passivity.

Having examined these possibilities using a variety of sources of data, only one explanation seemed to apply with equal force in all cases – that the processes of child-rearing, involving demoralization and feelings of powerlessness over the future of their children, had left mothers literally unable to see themselves as in any way actively involved in influencing events. With their sense of parental authority eroded, it became comprehensible that disturbing events in the life of the family no longer warranted 'getting worked up' since it would serve no realistic purpose. This attitude of resignation also had the characteristics of a self-fulfilling prophecy – the less often a parent thought herself capable of influencing events, the less often she tried and the less often succeeded.

This explanation also helps to understand why attitudes of resigned acceptance did not seem to characterize the fathers' responses in the same way. Fathers were simply less concerned with child care and, in the case of step- or adoptive fathers or cohabitees, were protected from child care by the concern of the mother not to impose on him.

> I'm the father, but you see I'm working . . . the mother, she looks after all these things with Margaret.

> Wife does all this . . . because I don't know a thing, me, because only thing I'm interested in is getting out and getting to work.

Thus, rather than relating to any gender-specific predisposition to become demoralized, fathers were simply protected (and protected themselves) from the repeated frustrations of child care.

As we shall suggest in later discussion, these attitudes of resignation in the mothers constituted in the social workers' eyes a considerable obstacle to effective intervention: they echo similar themes of resignation and apathy in work on attitudes towards the use of health services (Kosa, 1975) and towards the use of legal services (Morris et al, 1973), and in recent cycle of deprivation research (e.g. Blaxter and Paterson, 1982). In social work, as in these other areas, engaging the active participation of the client in problem-solving becomes a central issue.

The children's views

So far the discussion of the origins of care has focused entirely upon the parents' views and attitudes, while the part the children themselves played has been less apparent. This is partly a result of the availability of material. Owing to a variety of factors, children were noticeably less forthcoming about problems in family life than were their parents; standing somewhat in the dock, it seemed that children felt that they had most to lose and least to gain from going over the difficulties which led to admission to care, and their replies tended towards the monosyllabic and non-committal.

Some of the issues for children living in these families have been touched on already. Children were acutely aware of the levels of stress and of the allegations that they were its main source.

Child: Arguments just got worse and worse, so she said, yes, put him in care
. . . my mum were keen on idea because she were getting depressed and
that about me being at home.

Children were aware of the fragility of both their mothers' authority
and of the new family set-up. Consider this child's tale in response to an
invitation to describe how she came to be in care:

Well, my dad and my mum split up when I was three . . . and I don't really
know quite every side of the story because my dad told me some and my
mum told me some and, you know, you get a bit confused over which was
really the truth. My mum kept coming back and my dad kept saying that he
would have her back and then when she got settled in he used to chuck her
out again. There's six of us altogether and I've got three half-brothers and
sisters and our Terry, he's my half-brother, he was of my mum's first
marriage, he left with my mum because he was old enough. Then my dad
had loads of women coming in and out of the house . . . and he had one lady
and she had a son . . . Anyway, when my step-mum came along, she was still
married to [her husband] and her and my dad started getting friendly. They
got divorced and my step-brother, Steve, came to live with us and my dad
and my step-mum got married when I was six . . . I didn't like her very
much at all and I still don't.

This nightmarish account of the forming, disintegration and
reforming of the family constellation is offered as an explanation of the
origins of this child's entry to care. The reader will appreciate that this
tale is considerably shortened and cleaned up for presentation here; and
yet it is still extremely difficult to follow the exact changes in the family.
Imagine, then, the difficulties for the child herself in trying to make
sense of her experiences.

The issue of family reconstruction in terms, this time, of a father
leaving, also lay behind the following account by another child:

My sister left and me and my mum weren't getting on when she were there
but, since she left, that meant more work for me to do in the house, so mum
was getting on my nerves, I was getting on hers, then my little brother
started getting me mad and every time I shouted at him or hit him I got done
off me mum and then I got took to court for thieving from town, because my
mum weren't buying me nothing so I went down town and got stuff that I
needed and got caught . . . then my social worker said before court case
come up, she thought it would be best that I went into care and went to live
with my dad, so I was supposed to go and live with my dad.

Such accounts show how clearly these children grasped the stresses
on family life consequent on the departure or arrival of a parent figure.

Children also had opportunities to learn through watching the comings and goings in their own family, that one solution to incompatability in personal relationships was that one person should leave home. As the children above pointed out, they had seen parents, brothers and sisters depart in response to intolerable stress: sometimes step- or half-siblings moved between their parents, living with one until increasing stress resulted in departure to the other. This lack of cohesiveness in families and their readiness to allow members to leave surely left an impression on the children about appropriate ways of solving their own difficulties. 'Going away' was not, in itself, such a frightening thought as it might appear to an outsider.

Moreover, some of these children themselves had experience of temporarily leaving home prior to admission to care.

> My mother, she had a boyfriend living with her and I couldn't get on with her boyfriend, he kept arguing and fighting and that . . . so I told her that I didn't want to live here because of her boyfriend . . . just got to the point that I couldn't live here with him. That's reason why I went.

> I just couldn't get on with mum and dad and stopped out late, things like that and they ended up locking me out so for about five nights I stopped at my friend's house.

> Well, I were sick of my brother, we used to argue all the time, so I just ran away.

It seems likely that such experiences had the effect of further reinforcing the idea that departure was a viable way of solving incompatability in personal relationships.

It was also significant that the great majority (70 per cent) of children in the interview sample had siblings with either current or previous experience of care, a feature also reported by Berridge (1985) in relation to residential care. Some children also had friends currently or previously in care. Children could, therefore, conceive not only of leaving home as a solution but specifically of leaving home to enter care.

> I were glad I came in here, I like it . . . When I first knew I were going to come into care [my social worker] asked me if I wanted to go and visit it, so I visited and stopped overnight, so I weren't really bothered. I knew Deborah and Linda and Malcolm and Peter anyway before I came here. I used to knock about with this lass called Joanne and she used to knock about with Linda and Debbie and I got in with them.

It seems likely, therefore, that these children had learned ways of coping with stress which led them to be less resistant to the idea of leaving home than might otherwise have been the case. They had probably discussed care with their siblings and friends who had had experience of it, and were relatively well-informed on the range of provision and on the advantages and disadvantages of entry to care. The girl quoted above was 'glad' on entering care and 'liked it' and, as we shall show in the next chapter, the advantages in the eyes of the child of entering care over staying at home sometimes added impetus to the crisis leading to admission. It is important to grasp that this background knowledge of care, and awareness that departure of one family member was an acceptable means of resolving stress, apply with equal force to children who entered care voluntarily and to children who entered via the courts. We are speaking here of patterns of family difficulties which precede the particular events which lead to entry to care and are common across the board. As we shall show in subsequent chapters, these broad similarities in children's pre-care experiences, coupled with the haphazard manner in which the particular entry route is constructed, provide important clues to understanding the experiences of these children in care regardless of the actual procedures by which care was effected.

Initial contacts between workers and clients

The stresses and strains of family life described in this chapter inevitably coloured the communications between workers and clients. Initial contacts were frequently tense and fraught with the weighty backlog of information clients felt they had to convey to the worker, and it is time to turn to an examination of how the family's history was assimilated into negotiations.

Much of the tension surrounding negotiations between worker and parents over potential admission derives from the issue with which this chapter opened – the long history of the current difficulties. For the parents, the power and significance of the current crisis could only be understood against the backdrop of years of continual stress – the *'last straw'* effect. Acts of aggression against family members, destruction of property, shoplifting, truancy, suspected pregnancy, arguments – all these could be accounted fairly normal events in the lives of families, thus apparently rendering these parents' reactions extreme. Their attempts to compel social workers to recognize the burden of stress they had carried over the years was therefore partly an attempt to justify their reactions to current events.

In previous research (Fisher et al, 1984) we have commented on the importance of the concept of recognition during the early stages of contact between clients and workers. A fundamental characteristic of the different worlds of client and worker is that while, for the client, his or her problems are unique, for the worker they are commonplace. This inevitably produces tension in the early meetings between client and worker. The client is desperate to have the nature and history of the problem recognized and the consequent stress acknowledged: while attempting to offer this, the worker is also trying to categorize the client's problems so that his or her work becomes more manageable and so that the use of organizational resources, matching these categories, can be employed. This most difficult professional task for the worker can be understood as the need to hold constant the uniqueness of the client while simultaneously forming an assessment which will, to some extent, be routinized. Some commentators have stressed the value to the social worker of these routinized procedures (Giller and Morris, 1981) in terms of their defending the worker from becoming conceptually swamped by a plethora of unique circumstances. In our view this approach is only partially valid, since it overlooks the value to the client of this categorization procedure, which may bring access to resources and which may give the client some comfort in recognizing that problems are not abnormal in the workers' eyes. It also overlooks the extent to which workers may make a conscious decision to decline to offer recognition of the uniqueness of the client's problems, in order to avoid counter-productive emphasis on bemoaning one's fate (see Fisher et al, 1984).

This emphasis on the difficulties of the professional task in these early stages should not blind us, however, to the difficulties of the client's task. He or she must lay a claim to recognition of these important issues from the worker without generating antipathy and without giving the impression of total helplessness: the level of demand must be sensitive to the quality of interaction between worker and client so as not to provoke unwelcome reactions. This is not to say that clients simply raise the level of demand according to what the relationship will stand – such a view reeks of professional emphasis on clients' 'manipulation' – but rather to underline that asking for help from another person involves complex interaction skills, including the ability to read and predict others' reactions.

These issues are relevant to the negotiations between workers and parents over the nature of the difficulties they were experiencing. For the parents, the credibility of the worker was at stake. Did they have any children? Did they know what it was like to be a parent? Were they old enough to 'know a bit about life'?

> Mother: No matter how much training they've had, they haven't got kids, they haven't got the full 24 hour problem. They can't appreciate what you're going through.

> Father: [The social worker] is asking me to change straightaway . . . he wants his way, he knows it all, I know nothing. But trouble is, he doesn't know, like he knows everything in general, but I know my kids personally so I know there's some things they don't like doing, some days you've got to push them to do it.

As this father implies, it is also important that recognition is given to parents' detailed knowledge of their children as well as to their stress in dealing with the problems of children. This was a fine balance in the exchange between worker and parent – the parent had to emphasize both the pressure of parenting which necessitated external help, and the fact that the parent was still the most knowledgeable person about the child's needs. The expertise of the social worker in knowing children's needs was suspect if it derived, in the main, from 'books'.

These subtly conflicting pressures on the parent in negotiating with the worker were exacerbated by other factors. In presenting the demand for external help, the parent ran the risk of being thought of as totally incompetent, rather than as failing because of extreme pressure. Not only might the parents' special knowledge be discontinued, but so also might any further role for them in the child's future. When asked how their social worker might describe them, frequent emphasis was given by parents to the fear that they would be thought of 'badly' for having asked for help with their child; some parents went so far as to say they thought they might be described as 'incompetent', an 'idiot' or as 'ignorant'. Managing the exchange in such a way as to press home your demand without appearing incompetent or rejecting was clearly a skilful task.

The need for recognition of past pressure was overwhelming, however, and parents pressed hard for this in order to justify their reactions to the current crisis. In doing so they often encountered what was to them an infuriating response from the worker – that the behaviour of which they were complaining was only 'normal' and should be tolerated.

> Mother: [discussing her decision to press for admission] I don't know, I just feel that perhaps they don't think that Cathy is too bad and, as her parent, I do think she is bad and I wanted to do what was best for her . . . and I didn't feel I was wrong in asking for someone else to do this . . .

Other parents reported how, for example, the social worker 'talked them into' accepting that their daughter would go out for an agreed number of nights per week when they originally had hoped the social worker would reinforce their attempts to stop her going out so often, or how they were persuaded to let their son stay out late at night, despite their fears of his getting into trouble, because it was 'normal for his age'. Regardless of the wisdom or otherwise of this approach from the social worker, it is important to grasp how, in the parents' eyes, it reinforced their impression that the social worker didn't know much about children, didn't respect their detailed knowledge of what was best for their children, and hadn't recognized that this current problem was the latest in a long line of difficulties. Parents felt categorized as overprotective or rejecting, that their uniqueness was being overlooked as the social worker tried to 'play down' the difficulties.

Not surprisingly, some parents responded by pressing even harder, sometimes deliberately asking for help when their usual social worker was known to be unavailable in the hope of 'getting something done'.

> Mother: I've found that quite a lot of things in the past have been suggested but left until another crisis came up . . . and this is when I said it [admission] had to be done and had to be done quickly because again I was at the stage where I would have thrown Cathy out had they not done something very quickly, then it would have made somebody sit up and do something.

> Mother: At the moment I just give up. I was going to phone somebody else up this morning . . . He's [social worker] said to me many a time well when she's like this you shouldn't be on your own . . . if I was on the phone many a time, I says, I would phone up and somebody would *have* to come.

Thus negotiations were sometimes fraught with the tension of parents feeling they had to 'prove' to the social worker that their problems were genuinely serious and not just part of 'normal' growing up.

Underlying this tension, there was always the fear that the social worker's inappropriate emphasis on the normality of problems was a criticism of their parenting ability and an attempt to shift the focus of attention from the child to the parents. In fact this was a fairly realistic assessment of the social worker's approach. Consider the following descriptions of the same case:

> Child: My sister left and me and my mum weren't getting on . . . so my mum was getting on my nerves and I was getting on hers . . .

Mother: It started a few years ago [stealing money]. Cathy was eight at the time . . . she was buying sweets, perhaps this was to buy friendship . . . we were getting lies, everything Cathy came into contact with was destroyed . . . she's a child that's never been satisfied . . . disruptive . . . the problems have got bigger . . . they haven't gone, I don't know whether they ever will with her.

Social worker: Basically I think there has been a relationship problem within the family, or between Mrs Jeffrey and Cathy, for a long period of time . . . Mrs Jeffrey has never been able to acknowledge it as a relationship problem and has always seen Cathy as being deviant or at fault . . . What did concern me was that she did see her as devious, she did see her as terrible and refused to take any part in looking at her feelings on that.

The very accurate reading by this social worker of the discrepancy between her view of the source of problems and the mother's epitomizes the difficulties between the workers and parents; the social worker was prevented from being able to work with family relationships by what was seen as a 'refusal' by the parent to see the problem in terms of relationships. It is interesting in this case that the child's position appears to be closer to the social worker's than the mother's.

Other social workers had this difficulty; consider these four accounts:

Social worker (1): You see I took great pains to discuss with them that we weren't actually looking for an attitude change in Chris. You see what you often get is, right, he'll go to [remand home] and he'll learn his lesson and he'll be all right . . . I tried as much as I could to impress on them that that wasn't really what we were up to. I mean [remand home] wouldn't make Chris into a better person, it was up to much more changing in *their* attitudes to Chris and how *they* responded to that.
Researcher: How did they take that?
Social worker: Well, that's usually hard work, because although they all nod their heads . . . you find the next week, oh, he's been a lot better since he's been there.

Social worker (2): . . . my work is with Paula really, because it's fairly obvious that it's not going to work either with her dad or her mum.

Social worker (3): Superficially they seem to have had a lot of time and energy put into trying to prevent them ending up in care, but it probably wasn't directed the right way with the right emphasis.
Researcher: What would you say the right emphasis should have been?
Social worker: . . . I think the circumstances were adverse given the family

dynamics, but if greater emphasis had been put on trying to work with the family if it had been possible.

Researcher: You said earlier that you felt it was difficult to get on that level with them.

Social worker: Yes, it was difficult because it takes a lot of time, I think, and often it seems irrelevant to the parents and painful as well.

Social worker (4): I think they see our focus on talking things through with Karen and with themselves as being ineffectual, I don't think they see that as a particularly useful way of dealing with problems.

As would be expected, social workers took as a fundamental tenet that the genesis of child care problems lies in family relationships rather than in the intrinsic qualities of individuals, and sought solutions in 'talking things through'. Probably it would be safe also to speculate that preventive potential is ascribed to the opportunity of achieving an early emphasis on relationship problems. The frustration of this goal tends to be attributed to the parents' active unwillingness to see themselves as part of the problem; the word 'refused' used by one worker implies an active effort to thwart a particular approach.

It was clear that this fundamental discrepancy in approach was a considerable obstruction to joint work. In general, social workers were convinced that the parents' inability to see themselves as part of the problem was in fact defensive refusal and the possibility of alternative explanations was left unexplored.

Social worker: I see a lot of problems that the boys are experiencing as a result of tensions and unhappiness within the family but it's difficult to work at that level because I don't think the parents would accept that kind of initial analysis because they're rather mixed up about their own relationship.

Social worker: My original intentions were to work with the problems in the family and not feeling that I could have achieved that, perhaps the purpose changed partly because of the restrictions put on work in other areas, I think the purpose did change to Cathy. I think now again I have to say very clearly, both to Mrs Jeffrey and Cathy, that if I continue to work with them I had to spell out very clearly in what terms that would be, that it would be in terms of making demands on Mrs Jeffrey about areas that are very painful to her, that I didn't just feel that Cathy was the problem and that they were my terms of working and I really feel that it's taken the events that have happened for Mrs Jeffrey to actually accept that.

The possibility that parents might possess an alternative, legitimate view of the nature of family difficulties, or, as has been suggested earlier in this chapter, that repeated frustration might provoke a resigned withdrawal from seeing oneself as actively influencing one's children, did not form part of the workers' conceptual approach to these families. In a sense, workers located the inability to achieve a family focus in the intrinsic qualities of the parents, just as they often accused parents of trying to see all of their difficulties as arising solely from their children.

The attitudes of resignation discussed earlier proved especially problematic in the early negotiations between worker and client. Workers were indeed attempting to involve parents actively in the solution of family problems – 'pushing it back towards the parents' was a sort of byword for this philosophy of intervention. From the parents' point of view, however, this tactic could be just plain puzzling – why on earth was the social worker bent on involving them when, as far as they were concerned, the problems derived from inevitable processes beyond their control? Social workers without exception saw this response as defensive, as though the parents 'knew' really that they could have influence over events; little allowance indeed was made for the possibility that parents might literally be unable to comprehend this approach. It thus became possible for social workers to interpret the unemotionality of mothers as coldness ('She doesn't seem to care really'), and their unwillingness to take an active part in problem-solving as rejection. It was difficult to avoid the impression that psychological theories of family dynamics were often being uncritically applied, with the result that clients were pigeonholed as impossible to work with.

If initial contacts between clients and workers were complicated by lack of agreement about the meaning of certain emotions and attitudes, there were just as likely to be similar discrepancies over factual issues relating to family history. For example, all participants were asked whether the family had received help of any kind prior to contact from social services. Table 10 summarizes the responses from 25 families, six being excluded owing to missing data. (Note that this table uses the *family* [No. = 31], and not the *child*, as the basic unit.)

Families frequently felt that they had very little help of any kind prior to involvement with social services. Fewer than half of the client respondents recalled prior contact with another source of help. Echoing our earlier statements about the fathers' lack of involvement in attempts to solve the family's child care problems, fathers seem particularly likely to have been unaware of prior help.

In only one-third of families was there complete agreement about

49

Table 10 Levels of agreement about help prior to social work contact

Level of agreement	Child/SW	Respondents Parent/child/SW	Mother/father/ child/SW	Total
Complete agreement	No help ●	No help ● (7)		8
Agreement within family but SW disagrees	Relative/No help ● School/ Health Visitor ● No help/ Probation ● Don't know/ NSPCC ● Sister/Educ. & Police ●	Friends/No help ● No help/ Probation ●	No help/School and Probation ● No help/EWO ●	9
Disagreement within family but SW agrees with at least one family member		HV and Ed.Psych/No help/HV ●	Probation/No help/Probation/ Probation ● EWO/No/No/ EWO ● Ed Psych/Vol/Ed Psych/Ed Psych ●	4
No agreement at all		GP/No help/ EWO ● School/ No help/EWO ● No help/School/ Ed Psych ● No help/School/ Probation ●		4
				25

prior help – and in all of these cases it was agreed that no prior help had been available at all. In five of the nine cases where the family was in agreement but disagreed with the social worker, the only family member who responded was the child. In two other cases mother, father and child agreed that no previous help was forthcoming but the social worker mentioned help from other agencies. In all three of the two-parent families with disagreements, the father believed no help had been given, contrary to the mother's view. The four cases where all actors disagreed show very considerable communication problems. It is clearly unsafe to assume that all members within a family were operating from the same knowledge base.

Table 11 Levels of agreement about who first contacted family and community services

Level of agreement	Child/SW	Respondents Parent/child/SW	Mother/father/child/SW	Total
Complete agreement	Police • Mother •	Mother • (4) Court • Father • Police •	Court • (3)	12
Agreement within family but SW disagrees	Relative/GP • Father/Probation (2) • DK/ Court •	School/ Relative • Court/DK • Mother/Court • DK/Health Visitor • Mother/ Probation • DK/Court •		10
Disagreement within family but SW agrees with at least one family member		Mother/Educa- tion/Education • School/Mother/ School •	Court/DK/?/ Court • Mother/ Mother/DK/ Mother •	4
No agreement at all		DHSS/Mother/ DK • Mother/ DK/Probation •		2
				28

As table 11 shows, similar discrepancies arose regarding who first contacted social services (note here that we now revert to the child as the unit for analysis). In less than half the cases was there complete agreement. In the 16 cases where there was disagreement, some of the differences in perception were relatively trivial (e.g. where one actor could not remember or never knew). But more than half (ten) of these disagreements were of a more serious nature; in seven cases client respondents believed that a family member (normally the mother) first contacted social services, whereas the social worker maintained that referral was via an external agency. Clearly this issue concerning external referral versus voluntary requests for help could have been important in terms of the family's motivation, and it cannot but have been a handicap that there were discrepancies around this topic.

These examples demonstrate how easy it was for clients and workers to have different knowledge bases on even such relatively uncomplicated factual issues: small wonder that the difficulties of achieving a common starting point were exacerbated when dealing with broader issues in clients' attitudes and experiences.

Summary

We have drawn attention in this chapter to the ways in which the meeting of client and worker was actually a meeting of worlds: complex historical issues in the lives of clients had to be explored by the worker who was programmed by experience, training, and agency and public policy to be alert to some of these issues but not to all, and then to respond in certain ways. It is a problem of the meeting of a private individual with a public official, a meeting between the unique and the routine. A crucial aspect of this discrepancy was the clients' and workers' differing perceptions of the location of the difficulty. Where workers saw problems in relationships, clients, particularly parents, tended to see problems in people, a clash in perspective which led to fraught expectations and communication.

Thus, clients' initial problems in their meetings with workers lay firstly in ensuring that their unique plight was understood and recognized without falling into the trap of pressing their case so hard as to be seen as 'just another complaining parent'. Secondly, in pressing for action ('Something's got to be done'), parents were in effect pressing the worker to become an ally, to take at face value their assessment of the problem and to act in accordance with their wishes. Parents' negotiations were therefore characterized by tension between the need for action and for understanding.

This same tension also underlay much social work practice in the sense that, while attempting to recognize the need for immediate measures to change certain patterns of difficulties in families, the exact plan could not be determined without adequate appreciation of the nature of these difficulties. Put more simply, workers were under pressure to act without feeling sure of their ground. Experience, training and agency and public policy fell like a grid across the picture of family life which the worker was piecing together, dividing it into clear and manageable blocks which both resembled other cases in the worker's world (typifications) and led to discrete action (routine responses). Thus, parents who seemed inactive in the care of their children and unconcerned about their part in their future could be understood as rejecting: and this understanding led to the plan, for example, to minimize damage to the children by means of admission to care.

What this process overlooks, however, is that the picture of clients' experiences on which the grid was imposed was probably incomplete, and that, in any case, each discrete parcel of information is comprehensible only as part of the whole. Thus, the parents' sense of fatalism about their inability to influence events could be only partially understood as rejection – there *was* an element of rejection, but the full picture included a sense of loss of authority, of isolation as a single parent in the case of mothers, and of continuous stress. This full picture formed a backdrop to the current crisis, rendering parents' actions and attitudes more intelligible and the interpretation of simple rejection untenable.

Under pressure and in the face of demand to solve problems, it seems that social work practice was sometimes not equal to the task of managing the encounter between the discrepant worlds of worker and client. Often there was insufficient time to pay adequate attention to the history of the clients' problems, to issues of discipline and authority in the home, to parents' expectations of workers' intervention, and to establishing a knowledge base common to all participants. Too often disagreements about the nature of problems and about methods of handling them remained unexplored undercurrents in the exchanges between workers and clients. Too often, workers' and clients' views of each other concentrated on these mismatches at the expense of appreciating that there were considerable areas of agreement about the ultimate goal – a chance for the child to grow up, stop offending, start undertaking constructive plans for adulthood and so on.

Instead, social work practice tended to be somewhat inflexible and monolithic: under the pressure to take action, the scope for serious exploration of the origins of family difficulties became severely restricted and workers had to rely on only part of the picture, itself imperfectly understood in relation to the whole, as their information base. Unable to achieve a family focus, workers sometimes became frustrated and resigned to work which, in concentrating on the child, implied in their eyes that it was the child who had to change, even though their initial preference was to effect change in family relationships. Already the tide was running strongly in favour of admission to care.

4

Entering care

Introduction

This chapter concerns specific issues in the exchanges between workers and clients relating to entry to care. It focuses not so much on the events preceding care but on the issues around admission itself. It is valuable, at this point, to reiterate our approach (detailed in Chapter Two) to the 'obvious' external variables which are often assumed fundamentally to influence clients' experiences of care – the variables of criminal or non-criminal grounds for care, of entry via the courts in criminal proceedings or via an informal route – since it could be argued that the only proper method of understanding clients' experiences is to use such variables to pattern both data collection and analysis, using different interview schedules depending on the presence of criminal behaviour and/or a court appearance.

Briefly summarized, our position is that such an approach is wrong because it over-emphasizes a train of events which is only haphazardly related to the basic circumstances of clients' lives. Cicourel's famous study of juvenile justice (1967) and Parker et al's detailed analysis of similar issues in the English legal system (1981) show clearly that legal intervention is not consistently applied to juvenile criminal behaviour: rather a 'push-in tendency' operates to single out certain young people for prosecution quite unrelated to family and social circumstances. Moreover, studies of rates of detection of juvenile crime (e.g. Hindenlang, 1976) and of self-reported delinquency (e.g. West and Farrington, 1973) plainly show that criminal behaviour is a far more widespread feature of adolescence than statistics relating to prosecution would indicate: clearly the issue is not so much committing the crime but being found out.

Young people we studied demonstrated both these aspects. Some young people prosecuted and committed to care under S.7(7) (of the Children and Young Person Act 1969) pointed to their friends who had also been arrested for the same offence but who were not prosecuted. Some young people who admitted offending were committed to care via the courts for non-school attendance. Others who admitted offending had simply 'got away with it'.

For these reasons, and because of the way our initial findings directed us to examine in detail the young person's pre-care family experience regardless of his or her legal status, we have avoided using criminal behaviour or the legal entry route as a primary dimension for data collection or analysis. This is not to say, of course, that we have ignored this variable, rather that it features as one of many in appreciating why certain patterns of experience are found.

Parents' rights: a puzzle

The issue of parents' rights during admission to care illustrates well the virtues of avoiding a narrow approach to the study of clients' experiences. This was an extremely topical issue during the research: as a result of the publicity given by the National Council for One-Parent Families to a selection of cases illustrating apparent disregard for parents' rights over children in care, a bill was presented to Parliament by the Liberal MP David Alton. This bill was designed to reinforce the rights of the natural parents by ensuring proper consultation with them, particularly if permanent substitute care was planned. At the same time, a leading national newspaper published articles condemning the use of residential care for children, and the Law Society called for a reduction in the discretionary power vested in social workers to decide a child's future, and for an increased role for the courts. Social workers stood accused, it seemed, of undermining parents' rights by abrogating to themselves decisions which should properly be made in consultation with parents and possibly with judicial oversight. This particular swing of the pendulum in society's attitudes towards the public system of child care proved somewhat bemusing to social workers with whom we discussed this issue: they were, after all, developing their practice along the lines of S.18 of the recent 1980 Child Care Act. This section followed previous legislation in clearly giving first consideration to the welfare of the child. Suddenly the emphasis seemed to be changing.

It was in this context that we turned with interest to examine the views of parents themselves. As various commentators have pointed out (e.g. Hoggett, 1981; Dingwall and Eekelaar, 1982), the law is itself unclear on what are the rights of parents. Nevertheless, it was always our assumption in planning initial interview schedules that care would be seen by parents as affecting their rights over their child, however these were conceived. Although we were unsure how exactly to phrase the probe, experimenting with such terms as 'legal custody', 'rights' and 'involvement in decisions', we were in no doubt at that stage that we were exploring a perceived infringement of rights. Social workers' concerns also supported this assumption: we frequently encountered in social workers' accounts considerable sensitivity to whether the parents' sense of self-worth was undermined by admission of their child to care. Some workers, for instance, told us how they preferred parents to tell the child about admission in order to avoid further undermining parental authority; others indicated it was important not to be too specific about the location of parental rights in a care order for fear of eroding parents' sense of responsibility.

> Social worker: I don't think it's been laid down that we've got all the responsibilities because in some ways I think that would be a negative move really . . . I think they need to feel responsible because obviously she's going to live back at home . . .

It was somewhat surprising, therefore, to encounter an extensive lack of concern on the part of the majority of parents over whether care had affected their rights as parents. The sense of infringement was denied or the topic was seen as irrelevant. The apparent indifference of parents to this issue is well illustrated in the following quotes:

> Father: We have that little bit of power, they more or less run his life, as far as I know, virtually all the legal things that he has to do or whatever is their responsibility while he's in care. To me it doesn't really make a great deal of difference, if he's in care. I mean I suppose I could . . . probably go and . . . get him if we want, if we don't want them to look after him anymore.

> (To another parent)
> Researcher: Has anyone given you information about how things stand legally?
> Mother: Let's see if I can remember rightly . . . Yes, they did . . . if she came home within six months of being put in care, I could just go to the home and say I want my daughter back. But if it went over six months, then we've to go through some sort of paraphernalia. But even so, that question is not going to arise because she doesn't want to come home.

So striking was this indifference in the early stages of data collection that it was discussed in terms of possibly faulty question design. As a result, further probes relating to whether parents still felt involved in decisions relating to their children were added, together with a last resort question which bluntly asked parents who had legal custody of the child. These tactics still produced predominantly factual replies without any discernible sense of infringement and it was reasonable to conclude that we were knocking on the wrong door. The puzzle was: why was this the wrong door and was there a different door on which we should have been knocking?

In this sample we were frequently dealing with circumstances where one or other of the family members recalled having initiated the request for care: 17 of the 35 cases featured such a request. The departure of these young people from home was not necessarily, therefore, unwelcome to the parents nor, as we have indicated in Chapter Three, was it necessarily a radically new step or unheard-of for the children. Interestingly, in seven of the 17 cases where a family member recalled having originated the request for care, admission resulted from a care order, again demonstrating the danger of attaching deterministic importance to the social fact of an admission via the courts.

Rather than infringement, therefore, many of these parents instead experienced a sense of relief that their request for help had been heeded; that their child was sometimes also prosecuted was an issue which bore little relationship to any sense of infringement of rights. The intervention of others in their family life was positively sanctioned by some parents rather than regarded as unwarranted interference. This mother, whose son was admitted on a care order under S.7(7), gave a typical account:

> The reason why I got in touch with the social services, it was my husband works away a lot, well, I'm divorced, what with his drinking and one thing and another, I thought I was better alone. And it was just that everything was on top of me, it was during the summer holiday and he's a very, very highly-strung child and he just used to get me to such a stage, I didn't know what I was doing and this day he came in and he was crying for something or doing something naughty till I just lost my temper and I shouted with him to try and tell him that if he didn't get out of my way I would do something nasty that I would regret. And he wouldn't take any notice so I just jumped up and I ran him through the door here and he ran upstairs and I run after him, and on the stairs I kept my hoover and I just picked it up and I ran after him with it and I started to hit him with it, and if my daughter hadn't have been in the house, I think I would have done something that I'd be sorry for. Because he'd got me into such a state and he'd been like this for weeks and weeks, and then I realized what I'd done and I thought I've got to do something, I'm either going to kill him or do something silly to myself, which I didn't want because I love kids, I've always looked after them. So I just came downstairs and I thought there's got to be someone that can help me and then I heard about a neighbour who'd got in touch with social services with a little boy that she was having trouble with, and I thought

there's something so I just got onto the phone and I knew it was social services so I just asked who I could speak to and what I'd done. So they put me onto someone and they asked me the story of what had happened and I told them just what had happened that day, I says you've got to help me in some way, I live alone, I'm trying to bring four children up, I says, and this one is just getting me to a stage, I don't know whether I'm coming or going, I says I think one day I will do something that I'll regret. So they says well, we'll send someone to come and see you and they came about three days later.

In circumstances such as these, there was simply not the space to worry about whether the relief obtained as a result of the child's departure undermined one's rights as a parent.

Another aspect of parents' attitudes which reduced the likelihood that admission to care was seen as infringing their rights was a sense of lost authority over their children. As we have shown in Chapter Three, parents frequently felt that their children had largely escaped their control, and respected their parents less than a generation ago. This mother's reply to a question about whose decision it had been that her child should leave home gives the flavour of parents' perceptions:

She was so firmly fixed that, no matter what, she was not stopping here. It wouldn't have mattered two hoots what either of us said.

A social worker neatly summarized the situation in his reply to a question whether entry to care had affected the parents' sense of continued involvement:

I'm sure it did but I think they'd given up responsibility quite a while before then. I mean in the obvious sense, yes, they did become less responsible for him . . . but on the other hand they were saying quite a long time before we went there that they didn't feel any responsibility in the sense of being able to control him and didn't want that responsibility anyway.

It seems unlikely, in circumstances such as these, that parents felt that the process of entry to care significantly affected their rights, which they perceived as virtually eroded in any case.

For all these reasons, it seems that our concern, and the concern of workers, to explore how admission to care affected parents' perceptions of their rights, somehow missed the point. It was not that parents were unconcerned about the future of their children but rather that their anxieties did not centre on quasi-legal issues such as whether they were losing custody or control of their child. It is to an examination of the actual forms of their concerns that we must now turn.

Responsibility and moral sanction

In order to understand why parents' anxieties at admission did *not* centre on their legal rights, we found it necessary to explore how parents themselves understood their responsibility for their children. This process of delving more deeply into family circumstances *before* admission to care and of needing to understand broad issues in parenting in these clients' lives mirrors the process which we found necessary in exploring the history of the difficulties which led to involvement with social services (Chapter Three). This illustrates well one of the methodological problems in using the grounded theory approach outlined in Chapter Two: namely, that the pursuit of specific issues often throws up questions of a very broad nature, such as how parents see their responsibility for their children. These broad questions must be understood before the specific issue under examination can be accurately evaluated, and the researcher is faced with the necessity to broaden the scope of the inquiry beyond that for which funds and time have been allocated.

Fortunately, our research design permitted us to follow some families through several stages in their experiences of the public system of child care and these longitudinal cases (see Chapter Two) provided us with the opportunity to explore with clients some of these broader issues. Much of what follows, therefore, is based on data both from the initial interviews with respondents focusing on admission and from a second interview which, though concentrating on in-care experiences, allowed scope to pursue broader issues in clients' attitudes.

As we have mentioned earlier in this chapter, parental rights are not easily defined in law and, since it was an infringement of legal rights we first set out to explore, we thought it possible that we might have missed gathering data on perceived infringement simply because we had concentrated too heavily on rights as a legal issue. Indeed, when we took care to establish how parents themselves conceived of their rights, an entirely different concept to that of legal powers emerged.

Parents mentioned several areas where they felt they should have the right to tell their children what to do and be obeyed – such as friends, money, coming-in times at night, use of bad language and so on – and were quite clear that the way the child should be advised and the extent to which absolute obedience could be expected depended heavily on the child's age. Without it being requested, however, parents almost unfailingly added a justification for this attitude in terms of their *moral responsibility* to their children.

You've the right to influence them for their own good.

You've got to bring them up properly, teach them right from wrong.

Morally you have to let kids make mistakes so they learn.

After all, parents are responsible for their children.

You've to keep them on the straight and narrow, guide them.

You've a responsibility to make them independent.

Essentially parents seemed to be offering the view that rights flow from responsibility, the responsibility to care for, guide and enlighten their children. This responsibility in turn flows initially from the given biological relationship between parent and child ('He's mine after all's said and done') but can also derive from the sheer necessity for anyone living with the child to act in relation to immediate events – any adult *there at the time* was expected to accept the responsibility to act in the child's best interests and the right to intervene flows from accepting this responsibility. As we have seen in Chapter Three, there were some difficulties in families where one of the parents (or parent figures) was not a blood relative of the child and a degree of exemption from responsibility was granted in these circumstances. Generally speaking, however, adults were expected to take responsibility for children living with them – 'You've to teach them right from wrong, no-one else is going to'.

This association between given biological rights and earned responsibilities is crucial in our view to an understanding of parents' perceptions of entry to care and its legal framework. Responsibility for caring for children could very well mean, for example, calling in outside help.

> Mother: If I hadn't had her put away, she'd have still been the same. I don't think she would have altered at all and, to me, it's really best thing what's happened. I know it's rotten to say it, but it is, it's best thing what could have happened and I know she's in good hands.

> Mother: I did it more or less for her own good, not because I wanted to get shut of t' kid, because I didn't, but for her own good, so she'd make something of her life.

The issue for parents became, not so much whether entry to care infringed their rights, but whether it was consonant with their conception of their responsibility to their children, whether it was 'the best thing' and whether they were 'in good hands'. Of course, if difficulties had reached the point where a parent could not exercise proper authority over the child, it was logical in the parents' eyes to exercise responsibility by calling in external help. The issue then became how to decide whether the child was 'in good hands', and thus whether their duty by their children had been done. In the eyes of parents, 'in good hands' effectively meant being looked after by someone who accepted responsibility for dealing with children in the same way as the parents themselves would have wanted to take responsibility. Parents were looking to transfer the responsibility they felt to someone who would exercise the authority which they felt their child lacked.

> Mother: it's their responsibility because at t'moment she's in their hands, I'm not there to help.

> Mother: It's for control that they're in care.

> Father: It's to get them on the right track. I'd rather them go into care now than wait while they're 18 and end up in prison.

Parents' expectations of care revolved, therefore, around the issues of discipline and the exercise of authority. Their attitudes to someone else taking responsibility for this when their child was admitted to care depended almost exclusively on two things: whether the person doing the caring had the same basic attitude of responsibility as the parents and whether the actual authority being exercised was consonant with their notion of what the child needed. Rights were irrelevant to these calculations at this stage.

Clearly, in exploring the puzzling absence of a sense of infringed rights in parents' accounts we had touched on fundamental issues in the parents' concepts of parenting in exactly the same way as when, in Chapter Three, we examined the relationship between discipline difficulties, loss of parental authority and attitudes of resignation. We have here an inter-related set of issues concerning the family life of clients who are in touch with social services over child care difficulties. In order to understand any of the interaction between clients and workers leading to admission to care it is necessary to appreciate the context of such events in clients' lives. At the risk of repeating the message of Chapter Three, assembling all the parts of the picture often gave entirely new meaning to each individual part.

Not fully understanding the context of entry to care in the lives of clients, many social workers over-emphasised the issue of parental rights (as we had initially in the research) and energy was directed at sensitively handling topics which were not uppermost in parents' minds. Instead of concentrating on rights, parents preferred to evaluate the extent to which those offering help seemed to share their views of proper responsibility and the need for the exercise of authority. Their evaluation led to their approving or disapproving of workers' actions and of the care provided, irrespective of the legal basis of care – a process we have labelled the exercise of *moral sanction*.

The concept of moral sanction serves to explain the parents' concern that the nature of care offered to their child should match their perception of the nature and seriousness of their child's difficulties or behaviour. One remand home for boys, for example, with a reputation for strictness and toughness, was sometimes seen by parents as an extremely appropriate placement for a child who had repeatedly offended and needed discipline. This was what had been lacking at home, leading to the boy believing he could get away with misbehaviour: what was seen to be needed was a tight structure to which the boy would be obliged to conform, if necessary with a certain degree of harshness in order to 'teach him a lesson'. Conversely, placement in this remand home sometimes attracted the dismay of parents who felt that their child had not offended sufficiently seriously to warrant such strict treatment.

An assessment centre in frequent use for the children we studied was similarly evaluated. Its image in parents' eyes tended to be that its regime was rather soft ('They let them get away with anything up there') and parents would cite examples of what they saw as a laissez-faire attitude about coming-in times at night. The crucial issue here was whether, in the parents' eyes, the residential workers were in fact accepting the responsibility for dealing with the misbehaviour of the children in ways which the parents could approve. Perceiving an absence of this responsible attitude, parents did not feel that their child was in good hands and could not understand how this sort of care was supposed to help their child.

> Father: I actually said to one of the ladies in charge of Karen, from what I've heard, there doesn't seem to be any control over the children whatsoever. They're actually allowed to go out probably more often than ever they would if they were at home . . . The language to each other and to staff is just disgusting, they seem totally out of control.

> Mother: In the homes, they're allowed to get away with a lot of things. They

used to get up to messing about running up and down stairs, messing about and jumping on top of each other . . .

The evaluations of parents, therefore, focused on the extent to which the care their child was receiving corresponded to a pre-existing framework about appropriate ways of dealing with children. This framework was a product of clients' experiences, in terms of socialization and cultural expectations, of how you should treat children to achieve the desired goals of 'teaching them right from wrong' and 'respect'. A fixed repertoire of appropriate ways of dealing with children thus formed the psychological backdrop to the proposals of outsiders to intervene. This repertoire had probably grown up over years on an ad hoc basis and certainly predated the involvement of social workers. In response to various difficulties the parent experienced in dealing with children, he or she developed a set of practical measures which together constituted a pragmatic philosophy of coping with the demands of parenting. Such a philosophy ought to have incorporated flexibility and adaptability in order to cope with the changing nature of parenting as the child grows up. It is possible to speculate that lack of these qualities in their philosophy of parenting was a major reason for many of these parents' sense of distance between themselves and their children. Certainly our research would tend to point to a sense in which parents became fixed on certain responses to the problems children presented (particularly the 'discipline' response, but also the passive, 'it's out of my hands' response) and tended to take this as an immoveable reference point in any discussion of their difficulties.

Probably this evaluative framework had been applied to other proposals to deal with difficulties with children prior to those made by a social worker. Some parents referred to suggestions made by their own parents, by other adult relatives or by neighbours which had made sense to them and had been tried ('You want to tell that husband of yours to give him a good talking to'). Certainly, our own work and that of others (e.g. McKinlay, 1972; Stimson and Webb, 1975) points to the importance of clients' consultation with significant members of their lay helping network in the matter of whether to accept or reject the treatment or help offered by a professional (Mother: I asked me mum [about admission], and she said what else can you do?).

It thus seems probable that the framework of moral sanction constituted a touchstone for clients' reactions to advice. Proposals which had been tried before and seen to fail elicited a sense of despair in parents who expected something different.

Mother: [about workers' advice] But you know all this. You're trying to do that all the time, so nothing works.

New proposals, such as admission to care, were checked against prevailing opinion in the clients' lay helping network and against the parents' philosophy of child-rearing. If they made sense (i.e. corresponded to what parents and their relatives and friends saw as necessary), they were sanctioned and parents agreed, for instance, to the necessity to impose a structured regime on their child's misbehaviour, or to the necessity to explore whether someone outside the family could get through to their child. Crucially, this agreement derived from a positive sanction of the proposed course of action rather than by reference to any legal authority for its imposition: if the proposals made sense then the question of parents' rights was simply not at issue. Since we were mainly studying parents who were at the end of their tether, looking forward to the relief of having someone else try to deal with their children, working on the assumption that residential facilities would offer the kind of treatment of which they would approve (though they later questioned this), and sensing a loss of authority in any case, then the question of their rights was insignificant in comparison with their concern to ensure appropriate action was taken to deal with their children.

Workers' assessments of parents' attitudes

While parents were attempting to make sense of the interventions of social workers and the proposed care of their children, what sense were the workers making of the parents' difficulties and abilities during this period? As Chapter Three has demonstrated, workers were under pressure to act while possessing only parts of the total picture of information about families, leading to sometimes inadequate exploration of the history and context of the family's problems. There were, moreover, serious discrepancies of perception between family members, between families and workers and between workers themselves, even on relatively simple information issues such as who first contacted social services.

It is important to apply this context for understanding client-worker interaction to the issues surrounding admission. Of 17 cases, for instance, where the family maintained that the request originated from within the family, there were two cases where the worker maintained it originated from outside the family. Of 14 cases, where the initiative for care was seen by the family as external, there were three where the worker saw the family as requesting care. Although these discrepancies are small in proportion to the total sample, it is difficult to see how social work could effectively proceed in the context of such fundamental mismatches in perception.

Another instance concerned choice of placement. This is a complex area because there were different constraints on each participant's knowledge of the availability of placements, and we have no way of knowing from our data the extent to which clients' perceptions of choice related to the realistic awareness of the range of facilities which might have been considered. Thus a few children who knew of only one home and insisted on going there were apt to perceive this as having a choice. (For a discussion of these issues in examining clients' evaluations, see Fisher, 1983.) Nevertheless, the perception of having a choice (or of being obliged to accept others' decisions) relates importantly to the sense in which social work intervention proceeds by positive sanction or by imposition.

Fieldworkers were in the best position to make an informed decision about what influences had been brought to bear on the selection of placement. Interestingly, despite protestations in general discussions that they frequently wanted placements which were unavailable and had to settle for whatever was available, social workers mentioned a particular placement as 'selected' by this process on only four (of 31) occasions, and these were the only cases in which they did not see themselves as centrally involved in placement selection. In all 27 remaining cases, the fieldworker featured prominently, often in conjunction with the central administrative section for residential care (11 cases), in conjunction with the court (five cases), or with the clients themselves (five cases); in six cases, the fieldworker assumed sole responsibility for placement. Clearly, placement selection was seen primarily as a professional/administrative decision about the disposition of agency resources, involving consultation with colleagues rather than clients: this is borne out by the five cases perceived as involving client consultation which featured foster rather than residential care.

Clients had different perceptions of this process. Although agreeing with the central role of the social worker, clients were often completely unaware of the processes of negotiation within the agency or of the question of shortage of resources. Placement selection was thus more likely to be ascribed by parents to the worker alone (nine cases) or to the worker in conjunction with the court (seven cases). It can be argued that it is perfectly understandable that parents should be unaware of internal agency processes, but we would maintain that this lack of awareness probably reflected a choice made by the worker or the agency about the extent to which these agency processes should be revealed to clients, and thus constitutes one aspect of understanding clients' reactions to the service.

There were only two cases where a parent and a child respectively mentioned placement selection as a shared decision. Although there were no discrepancies between parents themselves, there were two cases involving discrepancies between their views and those of the social worker (one where the parents maintained placement was their choice, not the social worker's, and one where the parents maintained the decision was shared between the social worker and the court and was not solely the social worker's). There were seven cases of discrepancies between workers' and children's views: three where the child maintained placement selection was solely his or her choice, three where the child ascribed the choice solely to the worker (rather than to a shared decision), and one where the child saw the court as involved where the social worker did not.

Two important themes emerge from this attempt to enumerate discrepancies in perceptions over placement selection. Firstly, clients' ignorance of internal agency processes, whatever its origins, inevitably led them to focus strongly on the field social worker as the locus of decision-making. While this accurately reflected the workers' own perceptions of their centrality in this decision, clients tended to interpret this in terms of power to *control* resources rather than as a coordinating role. As will be explained in more detail in Chapter Five, when issues about the adequacy of particular placements arose, clients were not unnaturally disappointed to discover that the field social worker did not have the power to put things right by changing the way their child was treated or by moving the child to a different placement. Instead they were faced with the realities of resource shortages and a shared, consultative style of decision-making within the agency.

Secondly, children's lack of involvement in placement selection foreshadows a strong sense of powerlessness in the world of adults: they were least likely to have accurate information about the role of their social worker in placement selection and were least likely to perceive it as in any way *shared* with the social worker. This issue will be further explored subsequently in this chapter.

It has already been suggested (Chapter Three) that social work intervention was apt to miss the importance of discipline in the eyes of parents, and this had important consequences for workers' actions during the admission period. It should be noted, however, that 'discipline' is our word for the issue and we do not mean to imply that this word was constantly on the lips of parents we interviewed. Although some parents used related phrases ('a disciplinary care order'), few directly mentioned discipline and our use of the term must be considered as shorthand for the vast range of comments concerning children's behaviour and attitudes which parents felt were wrong-headed, demonstrated a lack of respect for authority and required firm handling.

It is the apparent lack of discussion of this issue which is puzzling in the approach used by social workers. In only about half the cases involving mothers did these clients recall any discussion of such issues as what methods are appropriate to handling problem behaviour. Similarly, most fathers and children could recall no discussion whatsoever of these issues. In reply to the same question, social workers claimed that discussion of this issue had arisen more frequently, although in over a third of the cases the social worker had not raised this issue with parents. (Sadly, we do not have data on discussion of discipline with children alone.) It follows that, on a case-by-case basis, there were more likely to be instances where the social worker claimed discussion of this issue where the client recalled none: but, paradoxically, there were also several instances where the client recalled discussion which the social worker denied having taken place.

Clearly it would be unwise to speculate on the meaning of such apparently contradictory case-by-case data. Nevertheless, at the global level, this material indicates a less than adequate fit between the workers' approach and one of the central concerns of clients in a considerable number of cases. Furthermore, parents' expectations of care were fundamentally related to their concerns over discipline and an approach which indicated no clarification with parents over this concern was extremely unlikely to lead to substantial agreement over the *purpose* of care. The door was thus open to discrepancies between workers and parents about what it was hoped care would achieve.

One obvious interpretation of the origins of such discrepancies was the possibility that, having attempted to open up the area for discussion, social workers met such an inappropriate insistence on the disciplinary aspects of care that they gave up hope of altering the parents' views. Describing just such an instance, a worker remarked:

That's usually hard work, because although they all nod their heads you find the next week, oh, he's been a lot better since he's been in there.

In work such as this, workers may well have felt that no furher purpose was to be served by resurrecting inappropriately punitive views: possibly it is in instances such as these that parents recall no discussion with the worker of their expectations of discipline in care. In other words, lack of clear agreement with parents over the purpose of care may well have reflected parental intransigence rather than lack of appropriate social work effort: lack of discussion of this issue may thus have reflected economy of effort, rather than ineptitude.

Two further issues were important in workers' assessments at this stage. Firstly, parents often described with some pleasure the first few days, or sometimes weeks, after a child's departure into care. Instead of a constant stream of minor crises, a relative peace descended and some parents relaxed in this relative calm. One father described his pleasure at being able to sit down to watch television without the fear of physical assault from his daughter; a mother was relieved that, as her daughter was in care, she did not have to worry at night, wondering where she was because she had not returned home. At first glance, such statements might appear callous and indicative of the shallowness of the bond between parent and child. Indeed, these were the interpretations generally used by workers. Yet such interpretations seemed to us to underestimate the level of stress parents had experienced, often over many years, from which it might be reasonable to savour some release. Such release was generally short-lived, not least because (as we shall show in Chapter Five) parents soon became concerned over the actual care their child received, and it was not so much characterized by a vindictive blaming of the absent child as by a brief, but enjoyable, rediscovery of very ordinary pleasures. The emphasis was on being able to watch television, or, as one father discovered, being able to go fishing again, rather than on 'it's only because so-and-so's in care'. To us, the workers' dismay at encountering these attitudes ran the risk of mistaking simple, temporary relief for permanent rejection.

Related to this was a second issue concerning the workers' estimation of parents' sense of longer-term responsibility. Workers were, in a sense, conditioned to see care often in terms of replacing an inadequate parent's inability to meet the demands of parenting. It was difficult for workers to see the patterns of parenting which had contributed to the attitudes in parents that care might be a positive way of demonstrating their concern to 'do right' by their children. In this context, there was, in the majority of cases, a tendency to see entry to care as marking a major shift in the parents' attitudes of responsibility rather than as another variation in a lengthy evolution. In a few cases, workers directly emphasized the benefits to parents of having a child 'taken off their hands' and spoke of their desperation in trying to get parents to 'accept responsibility'. Yet parents rarely gave evidence that a *complete* break was sought or that *total* responsibility now lay elsewhere, even though a few talked of the relief of handing over responsibility to someone else:

> Mother: It's best because since she has been away, it's been peaceful. I haven't had any upset and [brother] hasn't and you see [older sister] is working all day and dad's working all day, so they're not having it because she's playing up when dad's at work and she daren't do too much when he's in.

But the frequency with which a parent spoke of continued concern for a child's welfare ('I'm his mother, after all's said and done') showed that there was more to the responsibility of parenting than day-to-day care.

This discrepancy in perceptions should not be over-emphasised since, in terms of behaviour, there was a great deal of congruence between the parents' actions and the workers' interpretation of them. But beneath this superficial consonance there lay the seeds of important and far-reaching disagreements, which were later to emerge in relation to long-term planning and the appropriate extent of contact between parents and children, particularly where no return home was envisaged.

Young people's views: alienation and attraction

The young people's sense of being uninvolved in discussions with workers about the issue of discipline was an important forerunner of a broader theme of powerlessness – a sense of being unaware and uninformed about the actions of significant adults in their lives (including the social worker) and particularly about the formal mechanisms by which decisions were taken. Probably this theme taps the larger issue of the social role and treatment of young people, the extent to which our legal and moral stance towards them reflects natural justice and the lack of emphasis in our educational system on the nature of responsible citizenship. This wider backdrop, however, should not desensitize us to the acute helplessness and ignorance of some of our most disadvantaged young people. Consider the following description of entry to care by a young person:

> Car pulled up outside our house, I were walking down our street and he

stopped me and he asked me my name and address and all that lot. Anyway, he says I'm from social services and I says oh. He says how would you like to be put in care, and I says aye at first. Anyway he went to our house, he says just got to go back to your house then, then your mother can sign papers, put you into care, and I says all right, and I took myself off then.

Looked at from their point of view, the young people's frequent sense of uninvolvement in discussion of the issue of discipline, in placement selection, their sense of being pushed around by events 'out of the blue' and by the arbitrary actions of adults, and their sense of care as an indeterminate sentence (particularly, though not exclusively, when on a care order), amount to a substantial condemnation of our attempts to help children in distress, which it is difficult entirely to refute by reference to their inadequacy as witnesses to their own experience. More importantly, perhaps, this theme points to a sense in which the attempt to help these young people served to reinforce their sense of marginality, convincing them that there was little genuine care or concern available from the world of adults; it calls to mind the similar experiences reported by clients with mental health problems who, sensing their workers' unresponsiveness to their often ineptly expressed distress, felt confirmed in their view of the world as an unfriendly place in which no-one really cared for them (Fisher et al, 1984). Such feelings of powerlessness and alienation presage some elements in young people's reactions to care, particularly the extent to which they experienced the structure of residential care as concern or as arbitrary authority, which will be explored in Chapter Five.

Paradoxically, the prospect of care was not in itself particularly feared by young people. As we have indicated in Chapter Three, transfer from one home to another was often not an entirely unknown experience, and for some young people care had the particular attraction of a better material environment in terms of money, clothes, a room of your own and the high standards of accommodation.

> Researcher: What do you like about the assessment centre?
> Young Person: Getting spending money because I never had any when I were at home. Getting new clothes because I never had any when I were at home.

Care offered greater freedom than at home:

> Young Person: I didn't know anything about pop groups . . . I was in bed by nine o'clock when I was 14 and I don't have to be in till half past nine here so you can imagine the difference . . . coming up here and being allowed freedom.

Care also offered relief from stressful relationships with parents:

Young Person: When [social worker] mentioned it [care], well, I thought it would be a bad idea at first, but then I thought it might be a good idea to stop all the arguments, I weren't very happy at home.

Other attractive aspects of care included having your own room, more things to do, and, for some teenagers, the simple prospect of a roof over their head after ejection by their parents. If young people knew about care from older siblings or friends (70 per cent had siblings with experience of care), or had themselves been in care before (43 per cent had been admitted at least once before), they might bargain for a particular placement, or be in a position to weigh the advantages of admission against the disadvantages of staying put. It is important to understand that this sense of the attraction of care and of having some bargaining power can lead young people to say that the decision about entry to a particular placement was theirs, even when they have previously said how powerless they felt about the decision about care. Even in cases where entry to care was effected via the courts, it was possible for the young person to feel that care was attractive for the same reasons as young people who had not been subject to care proceedings.

The attraction of care did, of course, vary with the particular residential unit. Boys did not relish the prospect of enjoying the relative 'freedom' of the remand home, but they may have looked forward to teaming up with friends they already knew there and to the aura of toughness which might be ascribed to them by their non-care friends by virtue of their experience. Residence at a family group home led, not to an image of toughness, but to enjoyment of relatively greater freedom. Money and clothes were of course a universal benefit.

The attraction of care, combined with conditional acceptance that emotional problems may be solved by a physical move from one home to another, thus constituted an important dynamic in entry to care. The attraction of care should not, however, be thought of in absolute terms, but rather as reflecting the marginality and impoverishment of the lives of these young people. As a quotation above makes clear, it is the fact that care contrasts positively with the negative experiences of home which makes it, in *relative* terms, an attractive option. Few young people had any doubts about their choice if the option of their own family life had been available.

Summary

The theme that experiences of care are not primarily determined by the legal route of entry has been central to this presentation of the issues surrounding admission. It seems to us that there has been an over-emphasis on the issue of rights, fostered by the campaigns of various pressure groups and of the media, and a neglect of the question of the appropriateness of care as a solution to the difficulties of families. Certainly the parents we interviewed were intensely interested in the latter question and saw the former as a non-issue.

Social workers' concerns tended to focus on the question of rights and to overlook the central issue of discipline and the fit between the particular difficulty and the proposed solution. The reasons for entry to care were, therefore, insufficiently clear to allow joint planning with parents and the quality of communication was rarely such as to allow discrepancies in perceptions to become visible and thus susceptible to joint exploration. Again, the pressure to take action without time to explore fully all the reasons for it probably contributes to the selectivity of the workers' perceptions.

The concept that entry to care might constitute a variation, rather than a qualitative break, in the experiences of children of being cared for by adults and in the responsibility that parents felt towards their child, did not form part of the mental framework social workers brought to bear on the event. In relation to children who had experienced several varieties of family care, planning of the length of stay required and of the objectives it was designed to achieve was rarely comprehensible. Children's experiences of transition thus appeared to be encompassed within their general experience of feeling powerless in the world of adults; the arbitrariness of a move into care was often similar to the arbitrariness of the care they had experienced at home in terms of both its quality and the number of changes of caring adults.

In relation to the parents, workers consistently underrated the amount of continued responsibility and concern they felt for their children, tending to misinterpret relief as rejection and to give insufficient recognition to the value of continued contact between parents and children.

These differences in perceptions often seemed to us to be relatively minor and insidious; in cases where parents felt they had to present a crystal-clear case for their child to enter care and were now experiencing relief, it was difficult to see how a worker could remain open to the perception that parents had done this in the belief that they were acting in the child's best interests, and that they wanted to exercise some continued responsibility in relation to their children. In fact, however, these discrepancies were rooted in different concepts of appropriate parenting, and were to have long-term consequences for the children's experiences of care and for the parents' acceptance of care as an appropriate solution to their difficulties.

5

The experience of care

Introduction

This chapter examines the perceptions of parents and young people, field and residential social workers of the actual care received or offered while the child was in care. Its focus is residential care, partly because this was the experience of the majority (70 per cent) of young people studied at some time during their career in care and partly, as we have pointed out in Chapter Two, because 'genuine' foster care was under-represented in our interview sample. Residential care was also the focus of the parents' perceptions of what care consisted of ('going away'), and was one of the few areas about which young people talked relatively freely in our research interviews.

It is difficult, of course, to discuss residential care as an entity since, as Berridge has recently shown (1985), it encompasses a wide variety of units each of which possesses an unmistakable character. We will, nevertheless, persist with the concept at its general level because the numbers of young people in the interview sample would not allow us to build up secure pictures of all the different residential facilities and this would, in any case, distort their (frequent) experience of *several* residential units. It should also be remembered that many clients had only limited information about the range of residential provision and their views tended towards synopsis rather than specificity. Furthermore it is consonant with our research approach to question whether clients' perceptions are in fact primarily determined by variables such as placement; as this chapter will demonstrate, pre-care experiences and expectations seemed to us more vital in shaping clients' reactions.

Field social workers' views of residential care

If the field social worker tended to deplore the care the young person received at home and to look for someone to take responsibility for the young person in a way they thought parents were not, what did they intend residential care to achieve? Their approach centred on the themes of stability and structure very much as antidotes to the young person's experiences at home.

As Chapter Three has demonstrated, there was considerable inconsistency in the parenting children received simply because of the turnover of parent figures, particularly fathers, during the family's life. Added to this was the phenomenon of older siblings appointed to carry out parenting duties (Chapter Three). Thus, 20 per cent of the children had had to adapt to a step- or adoptive father, 60 per cent had lost contact with their natural father, while 20 per cent had lost contact with their natural mother. Such turnover inevitably led to the young people experiencing different philosophies and styles of management with little sense of continuity. Moreover, even within a single style of management, workers often pointed to considerable inconsistencies of approach, particularly as teenagers challenged parental authority. A typical cycle was described of alternating laxity and rigour, of a laissez-faire approach followed by punitive repression. Residential care thus offered the hope of establishing consistent management and a structure to the young person's daily life. The theoretical rationale was that the experience of consistent handling and of secure limits to acceptable behaviour would lead to internalisation of control by the young person.

Four field social worker (FSW) accounts:

In the short-term I'm trying to get [young person] placed successfully in a sort of stable way . . . and establish a routine. There's a lot to do in establishing a routine because it's been sadly lacking for a long time. There's some aspect of [him] being in surroundings and with people where [he] can try and learn to place some controls on [his] own behaviour.

There is a certain amount of rigidity and discipline there. I mean, they need the security of not being able to do exactly as they want.

It's a place where they are controlled to a degree . . . a place where they do have other controls which they haven't had at home.

I felt he needed a sort of total environment, where there would be key workers who would give him some structure in his life.

This theoretical rationale, it should be noted, was superficially very similar to that of the parents – the hope that firm handling would lead to self-control – and yet there was actually a world of difference in emphasis. On the one hand, workers emphasized the psychological needs of the young person for the establishment of security and internal control, in the hope of rescuing the young person from self-damaging patterns of behaviour, while, on the other, parents emphasized the necessity for a clamp-down to prevent further disruption to family and social life. This difference in emphasis, with its vastly differing consequences for handling young people, formed the focus of social work with many parents and gave rise to considerable frustration in workers at their failure to get parents to shift on this issue. It is possible, indeed, to speculate that it is precisely this superficial similarity in aims which leads to misunderstanding about the aims of care. Was it not true, after all, that workers were 'agreeing' with the parents' point of view by arranging residential care?

The fact that workers were arranging residential care was actually less positive than it appeared. A constant theme in workers' descriptions of their decision to admit the young person to residential care was that it represented *failure*. Their attempts to modify patterns of family behaviour had often been frustrated by parents' insistence on locating the problem in the child's behaviour (see Chapter Three), and shifting parental attitudes was described as 'pushing water uphill'.

Residential care thus came to be viewed as necessary only because of social work failure with the family, and a 'last-resort' attitude characterized workers' decisions to use residential care.

Nor did residential care often match the workers' hopes in terms of providing stability and structure. Workers often pointed to the fact that, while residential care did offer a great deal of structure, this was frequently unrelated to the needs of young people.

> FSW: There's a lot of routine there and things are organized for the kids and for the system and you will abide by the rules of the establishment and the rules are a, b and c . . .

Residential care thus stood accused of devising a structure to serve the needs of the unit rather than of the young people: instead of consistent handling, young people were subjected to regimentation. Sometimes this regimentation was felt to serve the needs of individual residential workers as well as of the unit.

> FSW: I mean, some of the things I've observed and some of the things [young person] has told me about the way some of the staff go on, is that they will use their power in that they will joke around with the kids and they'll reach a stage where . . . it can go one way or the other – if the adult pulls the authority, that kid is totally dependent and at the mercy of that adult. That's very unfair, it's abusing your position.

Rules and regimes thus ran the risk of institutionalizing staff inadequacy and idiosyncracy, producing insecurity and dependence in young people. This worker's perception of the position of the young person is strongly evocative of the young people's own sense of powerlessness described in Chapter Four, a theme which will be reiterated in their views of residential care.

Moreover, the arrangements for staffing residential units sometimes produced circumstances not unlike those from which the young person had been removed.

> FSW: The kids pick up if there's a lot of instability and chaos among the adult grouping . . . and I think a lot of kids get very unsettled because they don't feel that some of the adult staff actually have the ability to give them controls and boundaries . . . They have an awful lot of staff changes and it's bad enough I think for kids to be trying to relate to staff just going through an ordinary shift system without constantly having new people coming in.

Staff turnover and the problems of hand-over between shifts thus mirrored the young person's experience of parenting at home, and residential care was thus frequently accused of failing to meet even the minimum criteria for effective therapeutic work with young people.

Field social workers' criticisms of residential care were not limited to the lack of stability and appropriate structure. Complaints sometimes centred on the apparent intolerance among residential workers of disruptive behaviour, which was often seen as leading to recommendations for transfer, a process seen as damagingly mirroring events at home prior to admission. Where disruption included criminal behaviour, a recommendation for transfer to a more restrictive, penal establishment tended to be seen as an unnecessary further escalation of a young person's deviant career. Unease was also sometimes expressed at the way in which an established group of young people in a residential unit represented a closed social system, entry into which was a daunting task for a newly admitted young person (also seen in Berry, 1975). Occasionally, the reception from other young people was felt to be actually damaging to the young person. Lastly, workers often expressed concern over the ability and skills of residential staff in offering to a young person the psychological security of a significant personal relationship.

To these points it may be added that the data reported in Chapter Two indicates frequency of placement change as another ingredient in the lack of stability in residential care. In relation to their most recent admission, 33 per cent of children had two or three placement changes, and 17 per cent four or more placement changes. Social workers' lack of access to large-scale data of this kind on patterns of agency work, combined with the disparity between the duration of any single worker's intervention in a case and the total length of the child's career in care, probably accounts for the omission of this issue in workers' views of residential care.

The question whether fieldworkers' criticisms were well-founded or not is, in one sense, irrelevant to our research; that the majority of fieldworkers had a clear picture of residential care failing to provide some of the essential experiences which they had hoped to arrange for the young people they admitted, was enough to constitute a negative mental set towards residential care. It was a consequence of fieldwork failure and was therefore a last resort; it frequently did not meet their requirements, sometimes damaged young people and yet the pressure of family breakdown required its use. This negative mental set stood in stark contrast to the positive hopes and expectations of care expressed by many parents, and one suspects that this discrepancy may well have led to reluctance among workers to discuss openly with parents what residential care had to offer, when workers themselves often had serious doubts about its appropriateness. As a crude generalization, parents were travelling the road in hope while workers questioned its destination.

Residential social workers' views

At one level, residential social workers were in complete agreement with their colleagues in the field on the need for residential care to offer young people stability and structure, and they often focused attention on these as explicit aims.

Three residential social worker (RSW) accounts:

I sense we've gone through a rough patch . . . we've got her to hang on and she's still there, that's what we've managed and at times I didn't think we would.

I think we've helped her in the sense that we've stopped a bit of a sort of helter-skelter . . .

There have been some benefits because we felt he needed the stability . . .

Moreover, in fairness to residential social workers, many agreed with the criticisms levelled by fieldworkers, particularly the difficulties of achieving consistency between staff members and of compounding rejection in the face of behavioural difficulties from young people. Despite this measure of agreement in perception of the issues, however, residential social workers expressed fundamental areas of dissent, stemming partly from the lack of information-sharing by the fieldworker but, more importantly, from the different perspective derived from close daily living contact with the young people.

Residential social workers were frequently extremely poorly informed on the young person's background, the reasons for care and its purposes. The history of the family's difficulties, to whom parents turned for help, and what approaches had been tried and abandoned, were as absent from the residential social workers' account of the case as from the fieldworkers'. On these issues, it is not possible to say that communication between field and residential social workers was poor, merely that communication between both and client was poor.

But on the question of the reasons for care and its purposes, fieldworkers stood accused by their residential colleagues of unwillingness and inability to communicate effectively their plans, particularly where voluntary admission took place. Indeed, the accusation was sometimes made that no plan existed save that of depositing the child into care and retreating from active involvement. It is, of course, possible that their ambivalence about using residential care hampered fieldworkers' attempts to clarify to their residential colleagues what they hoped care would achieve. Probably this is rather generous speculation, however, in view of the difficulties fieldworkers had in generating clear plans: it seems more likely that the strongest element in the decision to admit to care, namely the realization that other options had dissolved and that care was a last resort, was in fact an *outcome* rather than a part of a plan for the future. In this sense, residential social workers were undoubtedly sometimes right in asserting that a young person had been deposited with them without the fieldworker having any clear idea as to the next step.

If a care order existed by virtue of a criminal offence, this at least gave a solid (though partial) reason for the young person's being in care and, at a very crude level, provided a focus for intervention – 'He's in here for his stealing. We've to stop him stealing and start him doing something worthwhile'. In these cases, residential social workers could at least see the logic of placement and could start to plan their own intervention. Fascinatingly, this sometimes led to fieldworkers complaining about the residential social workers not communicating their plans.

FSW: I was a bit concerned that what [remand home] were doing was hoping that he would settle. I felt they were perhaps hoping that he would carry on being settled and that by the time it got to the review, they could say, well, this lad's been here for how many months, he's got a job, he's not been in any trouble, things are going well, we think he should go home. And I would have resisted that, even if things had been going well.

Where residential social workers felt that the fieldworker had no clear plan, or had failed to communicate it, it is hardly surprising that they sometimes began to generate plans independently of the fieldworker. This tendency mainly originated, however, not from lack of communication but from a fundamentally different perspective on the problem, deriving from the demands of residential work.

As many commentators on residential work with children have pointed out (e.g. Berry, 1975), close daily living with children who have developed patterns of disruptive behaviour and suffered a degree of parental rejection resembles constant psychological assault. The client's behaviour is often designed continuously to test the worker's responses, to provoke familiar reactions to which counter-reactions come easily; in short, to replicate the sort of relationships which led to family breakdown. Residential workers were quick to point out that the necessity to react appropriately to young people during the lengthy contacts of daily living was quite different from the fieldworker's experiences, and required day-by-day, and sometimes hour-by-hour, planning rather than six-monthly reviews. Residential social workers maintained that group living in residential care *necessarily* generated plans because of the need for strategies for managing behaviour here and now. This fact of residential care affected planning in two ways. Firstly, the residential units developed regimes independent of young people's needs; these were necessary to ensure the functioning of the unit and required a degree of conformity from all residents. Secondly, the young people lived in groups (often several groups within a single unit), and the residential social workers had to consider the needs of the group as well as of the individual young person. It was thus naive, according to the residential social workers, for fieldworkers to expect that care could be uniquely tailored to a particular young person's needs: there were always certain house rules or group needs which had occasionally to take precedence.

An example of this discrepancy concerned a young person for whom the fieldworker hoped care would offer the opportunity to vent some of his anger at the way he had been treated at home, and thus to become more open and expressive about his feelings. The fieldworker was disappointed to find that care did not achieve this and felt that the residential social workers were to blame for being 'afraid to help his anger out'. The residential worker was aware of this need but judged that the group of young people with whom this person lived did not have the resources to cope with his anger if its expression was encouraged. Such disparity in approach should of course have become the focus for discussion so that the resource of residential care could have been used for what it was capable of achieving, rather than blamed for not achieving what was deemed impossible. That it was not openly discussed, the young person later leaving care to return home in circumstances not dissimilar to those surrounding his admission, demonstrates the barriers to understanding between residential and fieldworkers which often prevented a cohesive approach.

The philosophy of residential care was not wholly reactive to the demands of daily living, of course, and it is time to turn to an exploration of some of the broader themes in residential workers' accounts. As other commentators have pointed out (Parker, 1978; Packman, 1981), teenagers place different demands on residential care. Partly because of long stays in care resulting in an increase in the average age of children in care, and partly because of different patterns in the use of the range of care options resulting in a decrease in admissions to residential care of younger children, residential workers who entered the service some years ago, expecting and trained to deal with the under-tens, now find themselves increasingly dealing with teenagers. This broad outline of changes in the national picture was roughly paralleled in the host agency, with the result that the age profile of the in-care population (excluding those at home on care orders) peaked at 15 years.

While it would be wrong to suggest that residential workers had not adapted to the differing demands, the philosophy of an earlier generation of child care was deeply ingrained and still underlay some of the basic structures. For example, the form fieldworkers completed about the young person in order to give the residential social worker information, centred on the physical needs, likes and dislikes it was more appropriate to know in respect of a toddler than a teenager. Some residential workers' accounts appeared to describe an attempt to create a homely atmosphere in the residential unit and criticized young people for not making enough of an effort to make their rooms their own.

His room is always immaculate, that worries me. He's nothing at all on the walls and I keep saying to him when are you going to brighten this room up a bit with a few posters, but no, he doesn't want to. Very stark.

There was evidence that some residential workers were still known by their teenage clients as 'auntie', betraying an outmoded attempt to reassure young people by introducing pseudo-family relationships into professional caring (hence such terms as 'housemother', 'housefather'). In short, there were some signs that the care-as-compensation philosophy was still central to residential social workers' understanding of their role. Thus, a child who was perceived as deprived of normal family life was given compensatory relationships within an environment made to resemble a home-from-home in the hope of minimizing psychological damage. As we shall see in examining young people's responses, such approaches often hit exactly the wrong note.

Two other significant strands in residential social workers' accounts were the attempts to introduce a new philosophy in keeping with the changed nature of the task. Several residential social workers mentioned de-institutionalization as a general goal of relevance to the young person's needs.

> RSW: Some units operate rota systems as far as washing-up is concerned, we don't, the reason being we want to get away a little bit from institution. You can never replace a home but we can try a bit and make it as homely as possible.

Deinstitutionalization thus appeared to mean the removal of routines which prevented young people from learning that cooking, cleaning and washing were necessary parts of daily life in which they had themselves to become involved and to develop skills. Related to this concept was the second strand of independence training.

> RSW: Basically we are getting them ready from the age of twelve for independence, whether it's semi-independence or total independence, even though some of the kids may be returning home, we still consider that they should have the skills to be independent if necessary, and that is what this unit is geared to do.

Young people were thus regarded as no longer needing to be protected from the demands of daily living, but rather encouraged through skill training to master the tasks necessary to their eventual independence.

Though these were undoubtedly appropriate moves to reflect the older age range of young people in residential care, several issues of implementation arose relevant to our focus on perceptions of care processes. Normalization tended in practice to be only partial – the child was asked to clean his own room but not to shop for the daily provisions – for the obvious reasons that cost-effectiveness and benefits to clients are not synonymous. Within the setting of local government institutional care, some activities are more cheaply carried out on a centralized basis and this requirement overrides the need to help young people to become involved in the practicalities of their care. On the other hand, some activities, if easy to devolve on the young people, are attractive not only because of the benefits to clients but also because of financial savings. Money for shopping is not so easily made available to young people as are a dustpan and brush.

Moreover, this policy encountered some resistance among young people we studied; a consumerist approach led a few to point out that residential workers were being paid to care for them, and should get on with it and not expect young people to make their job easy for them. It is easy to see how, living within a society which emphasizes value for money, young people could arrive at this misunderstanding.

Independence training was not without its drawbacks in terms of its relationship to the fieldworker's plans and the overall pace of the young person's progress. We encountered an example where the fieldworker was planning a young person's return home, while the residential social worker was undertaking independence training; such an approach could have been consistent with a short-term return home and the need to increase the young person's living skills. In fact, the residential social worker was simply ploughing ahead because this was her job in the residential unit and the appropriateness of including this specific person in the programme had not been explored.

Another example concerned a young man who stood to inherit money and was banking on this to set him up on leaving care. He too was included in an independence programme, while protesting that he didn't need the skills as he would be able to pay someone to look after him. Clearly such programmes sometimes ran the risk of being applied before the counselling work had been undertaken to prepare young people psychologically for independence; the danger was that teaching a young person to use a washing machine was much easier than tackling his fears, anxieties and insecurities about psychological survival on his own.

In summary, the approach of residential workers did not fully correspond with the task of dealing with an older age group. Despite some areas of agreement with their fieldwork colleagues, residential social workers tended to operate from a different perspective and set of priorities and there appeared to be considerable problems in achieving a coherent service involving field and residential work.

Parents' hopes and disappointments

It was noted in Chapter Three that parents often feared that their children might be led astray by other children, particularly if they spent too much time on the streets. Much effort was thus expended in attempting to control the amount of time children were exposed to 'danger on the streets'. This frequent fear that their children might get into bad company and be seduced into delinquent behaviour by the gang mentality grew stronger the more parents learned about residential care. It was here, of course, that these 'other children' had ended up and, far from preserving their children from bad influence, residential care tended to be perceived as enforcing full and damaging exposure.

> Father: I wasn't impressed at all. They were older than what he was. It was a shock because they was rough, there's no doubt about it.

> Father: She's been, for the first time in her life while she's been associating with the children there, they took them out on a day trip to a market centre somewhere and they've come back with, her and two other girls have come back with stolen articles of clothing, skirts I think they were.

One of the dominant disappointments among many parents was, therefore, that residential care *contaminated*.

During their visits, parents tended to pick up selective bits of information about the behaviour of the children in the residential unit. These partial items of information fed their fears about contamination. A father reported hearing a young person swear at a residential worker and noted that the residential worker did not react but continued his discussion. A mother saw young people climbing on the roof during one of her visits. Another watched a young person cheeking the staff, again without apparent staff reaction. A widespread feature of parents' accounts of residential care was thus disappointment at the lack of control exercised by residential staff, who appeared to the parents to be too passive, soft and laissez-faire.

This apparent laxity in residential care was exacerbated by what was perceived as the inappropriate degree of freedom permitted to young people. A mother who had feared prior to her daughter's entry to care that she would 'get into trouble' through staying out late, found that she had on occasions been given a key and told to let herself in at night. Often, the young person was seen to have greater personal freedom to come and go in residential care than at home. Even in the remand home, where this personal freedom was not permitted, parents sometimes expressed dismay at the fact that their son was allowed to smoke when he had been discouraged at home. This sense of frustration at their child receiving increased freedom when the parent had expected some form of discipline is well illustrated by one father's reaction:

> [FSW] thought it was the best place for [young person]. But after looking at what they've been doing, I don't think it is. They let him do what he wants. I mean, he's dying his hair green and black and all sorts and I've gone barmy with him about it but . . . I don't agree with letting 13 years old kids smoke, which they do do . . . There's no discipline up there at all, they're just running wild, they might as well be at home.

Moreover, parents sometimes felt that the lack of discipline in residential care was such as to further undermine their own authority, and the perceived unwillingness of residential social workers to exercise control created more difficulties at home.

> Mother: He's cheeked his father once or twice when he first come there . . . in fact he once slammed door in his face. His father got hold of him, he says I don't care what you say, you might have done it up there but you're not doing it here.

This perception of laxity in exercising control over young people applied to all types of residential care, from the remand home to the smallest family group home, and clearly related to parents' initial expectations of what care would provide. If parents were looking to hand over some sort of responsibility for day-to-day care for their children to the residential worker (Chapter Four), their reaction was overwhelmingly one of disappointment that the staff seemed unprepared to tackle the children in ways of which they approved. The staff just did not seem to accept this 'living-with' responsibility, the duty as a responsible adult to intervene, set limits, control and guide youngsters: the philosophy appeared instead to be one of 'just letting them get on with it'. A widespread feeling among parents was thus that they had been *misled* in their expectations of residential care. The moral sanction for intervention (Chapter Four) was, therefore, wearing thin, and parents' disillusionment often led them to reconsider whether they should permit their children to continue to stay in care.

Parents' reactions were varied, although a general impression was gathered that the research interview provided a rare occasion for them to voice their feelings on this issue, implying that it was difficult to raise with their workers. Sometimes, parents took bitter comfort from the fact that the residential staff were, in their eyes, doing no better than they had when the child had been at home. It was thus possible for some parents to feel vindicated in their perception that it was the child who was the problem. Other parents made lengthy and frustrating attempts to convince their field social worker of the problem and to enrol an ally in persuading the residential social workers to react differently, or in arguing for transfer to a different unit. In doing so, these parents, of course, ran the risk of being told (or of succumbing to inner voices of guilt) that if they did not approve of what was happening they could have their child home again.

It was at this stage that the legal status of care began to be reflected in parents' reactions. There was clear reticence, or guardedness about their *right to complain* of the standard of care, among parents whose children were subject to a care order. It was not that parents felt they had not the right to be concerned about the care of their child, but rather that the existence of a care order was felt to cast doubt on their qualification to know what was best for their child. Such parents tended to look to the expected length of the care order and to the possibility of a move to another residential unit.

Such reticence was far less marked in parents whose children were not subject to a care order. These parents' views were more strident and scathing about the quality of care and about the perceived inexperience of some residential social workers. In an extreme example, these findings led one mother to visit her daughter's residential unit and make a take-it-or-leave-it, last-ditch offer to have her home in the hope of preventing further damage. The following day, on stringent conditions, her daughter returned home.

What is signally lacking in the parents' accounts is any sense of having shared this concern with the residential social workers or of having been consulted by any worker about the aims and methods of residential care. It is possible to speculate about the reluctance of parents to criticize those in whose care they had agreed to place their children, particularly if a care order had been made; caution was required in managing their parental image in the eyes of the workers in case their complaints be taken as evidence of ingratitude, or, worse, of inability to comprehend what was best for their children and thus potential disqualification from their further care. Although this reluctance was probably an important factor, more significant was the apparent lack of any formal attempts by workers to communicate with parents. Field social workers often appeared in the parents' eyes to know little about the ins and outs of the residential units and their role as an intermediary did not feature strongly in parents' accounts. Nor was it clear to parents which of the many residential workers they were supposed to talk to about these issues: a few parents remarked on the (to them) extremely junior status of a residential social worker, and declined to discuss their complaints at this level. Parents did not always appear to know when they could contact a residential social worker, or if there was a meeting on a regular basis which they could attend.

In other words, although parents' reluctance, ambivalence or (sometimes) apathy was instrumental in creating their sense of alienation from the care being given their child, so too was the apparent absence of easy opportunities for communciation, either through informal relationships with staff or through formal arrangements. The saddest example of this lack of communication concerned a teenage girl who was admitted voluntarily to residential care and, after a couple of weeks, began to complain that her parents never visited and were rejecting her. When the parents eventually visited, the girl's angry reaction provoked the father to threaten never to have her home again, while the mother's sense of failure grew. The residential social workers were not particularly surprised at the parents' lack of visits, which they put down to rejection, and laid plans to start independence training. The issue of lack of visiting was raised in a subsequent research interview with the parents, in which they revealed that they had discussed together how to handle the transition to residential care and had decided it was best to avoid visiting the residential unit for a couple of weeks in order not to interfere with what they were doing. No-one appeared to have helped them to plan this tactic and no easy channels of communication were available to point out its dangers. This misguided concern thus backfired and created further distance beween parents and daughter.

Young people and arbitrary authority

It will be remembered that the decision in favour of entry to care often had an out-of-the-blue quality for young people, even where the decision arose from a court appearance. This empha zed to young people their uninvolvement in decisions and their powei essness in the face of the (to them) random, arbitrary and inconsistent actions of adults. It was this sense of having to adapt to the rules created by adults which was one of the most salient issues reported by young people about their experience of care.

> Researcher: How do you find out how the place is run?
> Young person: They don't explain anything to you, you have to find out yourself.

Researcher: And how do you find out?

Young person: Just watch what others do.

Researcher: Is there anybody you can ask or does it feel a bit strange to ask what you're supposed to do?

Young person: You feel daft asking so you just watch what they do.

Consider another young person's views:

It were about two weeks after I actually went in before I knew all the rules. You pick things up anyway, and kids tell you, don't do that, you'll get into trouble.

This process of 'wising-up' was felt to be somewhat unfair, since it seemed to them that they were not being given clear instruction on what was expected. It should also be noted that many of the formal rules touched on issues which had also been contentious at home (such as when to come in at night or smoking); thus any contradictions in the regimes stood out in stark relief.

What was even more unfair in the eyes of young people was that, in addition to these formal rules, they had to contend with the idiosyncratic ways in which they were applied by staff.

Young person: When [you] first come in [you] have to watch what you're doing, because you have to get to know staff really well . . . You don't know the rules when you come in and you don't know the staff and they don't know you. You don't know what to expect off staff and they don't know what to expect off you . . . [You mustn't] mess about a right lot, I mean until you get to know them because . . . most of staff, they mess about with you but up to a point like.

Researcher: Is there a point you're not really supposed to fool around beyond, is that what you're saying?

Young person: Yes.

Researcher: How much can you fool around?

Young person: I don't know but sometimes when we're all watching telly and somebody comes on that we don't want to watch and one of staff does, we throw cushions at them or something like that, that's all right but when it comes to knocking things over and things like that, it's a bit much then.

Each staff member was seen as having a personal approach which the young people needed to appreciate in order to avoid unwitting transgression. Tailoring your behaviour to the estimated tolerance of the staff was a tricky enterprise: some got it wrong.

Young person: A couple of months ago, just coming in from work, went downstairs to get my tea, no tea saved for me, so I goes upstairs to sit down and this kid hit me on head with a comic or something so I jumped up and threatened him like, and one of staff says come here, I want a word with you, stop messing about, so I were mad and just said you can't even just come in from work, can't even watch telly without somebody hitting you over head with a bleeding comic and I says I just don't want to listen to what you've got to say and I just went in and sat down. He says your weekend's stopped.

That different staff members were seen to apply the rules differently was well documented in our interviews with young people in care. Staff had favourites:

Young person: A certain member of staff will like a kid better than anybody else and give them extra privileges and all that, and I think that's wrong.

Staff could be seen as petty:

Young person: I mean, the other day, I said can I have 5p for the disco out of my pocket money, then she were going off about her only being able to save 95p instead of £1 if I had this 5p. And I says, well, can't I have it then, then she starts shouting at me because I didn't say, can I have it please.

Staff members contradicted one another:

Young person: One of them might tell you to do something and you get told off by another staff for doing that, so you don't know where you are.

That the rules themselves were seen as inconsistent is also well documented. They seemed too fussy, and ad hoc:

Young person: There's a new rule come out every time somebody goes in, always. My mate, he could smoke when he were 15, just got to his fifteenth birthday, then they changed the rule again saying you had to be 16. Then somebody else came in, there were another rule out, but they hardly ever told you about any of the rules.

They had inappropriate blanket sanctions attaching to them:

Young person: Say if there's like three kids talking when they've told them to shut up, they should tell them off, not everybody. One kid takes a drag of someone's cigarette, then staff stops everybody's cigarettes for a week. Shouldn't do that, it's not fair.

It should not be forgotten that many of the young people had frequent placement changes and thus had to adapt to different regimes. This was well described by one girl in relation to a new entrant to her family group home:

I mean, we've got this new boy, he's come from [remand home], he's all right, you know, he's probably got his problems but to tell truth I can't stand him. He walks around with his belt and he snaps it like this . . . Perhaps in [remand home] boys go round jumping on you round corridors but we don't go round doing that and we try telling him that but he can't get it into his head . . . , I mean, in [remand home] perhaps there the more crime you've done, the better you are . . .

The picture pieced together depicts the essentially *arbitrary* nature of the authority exercised by adults. Formal rules are difficult to get to know while there are extensive unofficial norms set by staff in their interaction with young people. This interaction was characterized as a difficult exchange involving estimating the tolerance of individual staff members and gauging the corresponding limits of behaviour. Usually this arbitrariness was seen as nothing more than a pervasive feature of adults, but sometimes it was felt to be malevolent.

> Young person: Some staff push you around and I say I bet you don't go round streets doing that to men of your own age, your own size, and you're just taking advantage of your job . . .
> Researcher: So you think they've got too much power, then, over the boys in here?
> Young person: Mm, a lot too much. Say if you're trying at football or cricket and staff don't think you are, then they'll say if you don't start trying then we'll stop your cigs . . .

This perception was rare, however, and seemed to be limited to describing interaction between male staff and boys in a remand home.

The characteristics of arbitrary authority bear considerable resemblance to the fieldworkers' reservations about the opportunity in residential care to ensure stable and consistent handling. Although the young people's views were inevitably more personalized and vociferous, both emphasized the injustice of subjecting young people to what is perceived as poor quality care, a feature central to the wider protest movement involving young people in care (the 'Who Cares' movement, see Page and Clark, 1977). A further similarity between the views of young people and fieldworkers concerned the need for structure. Both were at pains to emphasize that structure and control, on a consistent basis, should be the aim, and young people certainly did not object to strictness in itself. Only when the strictness was seen as inconsistently or unfairly applied was it wrong.

> Researcher: What about [residential social worker], what's he like?
> Young person: Can be strict, he's fair . . . In a way they're too soft, they should be a bit stricter, but they shouldn't stop everybody's privileges over one person.

Indeed, fairly exercised, strictness could be seen as the guarantee of justice.

Clearly this implies that the young people were not unaware of the demands of life in residential care, and possibly that they had some inkling that clear structure and control might be in their individual interest. It is equally clear, however, that an essential theme in their relationship to the adult world, generated by events prior to admission, had largely been reinforced by their experiences in residential care – that authority exercised by adults was unjust, arbitrary and commanded tribute but not respect.

The philosophy of care as 'home' provided a second common link between young people in their reactions to care. If living at home was intolerable to some because they felt constricted by petty rules, and if residential care was attractive partly because of the hint of increased freedom, young people sometimes felt extremely angry about any attempt to mimic family life. This was experienced as pressure to contribute to the overall sense of group support, pressure to demonstrate a sense of belonging to the unit and pressure to regard staff as substitute relatives. Teenagers in particular worked hard to avoid the feeling of being obliged to help their fellows in the way siblings would have (sometimes) helped one another; they resented questions about why they had not even put up posters in their room to make it more 'homely', more 'theirs'; and they ridiculed the idea that they should regard any staff member as a substitute parent or 'auntie'. As one boy put it 'This isn't my home – I've got a home.'

Such behaviour is, of course, open to alternative explanations: residential social workers typically saw defensiveness and insecurity in these responses and continued to offer parental warmth in order to demonstrate their readiness to accept 'difficult' behaviour. Although not wishing to discount the possible validity of this approach, in our view it over-emphasised the need to provide emotional compensation to young people and underestimated their capacity to make independent plans for emotional survival. Any relationship with overtones of parenting ran the risk of being rejected through association with the theme of authority, and our impression was that relationships with these young people were perceived as more appropriate if the helper's behaviour and attitudes resembled those of an older sibling rather than those of a parent.

The final issue in this theme of arbitrary authority concerns the young people's views of their fieldworkers. Although little general impression of the perceived purpose and value of a fieldworker's contact could be gained, young people were freely critical of its timing and reliability. One described how, on learning that his social worker was to visit but not at what time, he spent all day waiting for her arrival in the late afternoon: he maintained, not unreasonably, that he could have spent the time more usefully. Another described how his social worker would always arrive on the school's games afternoon, so that he never got an uninterrupted football match. Although these complaints concerned a minority of the young people, the effects on their perception of the social worker were considerable.

What is striking about this issue is that the social worker's visit warranted such prominence, either by the staff requiring the young person to give it precedence over the routine requirements of residential life, or, rarely, by the young person's ascription of significance. These visits did not seem integrated in any way into the normal flow of the daily residential experiences and no feedback channel appeared to exist to recognise and communicate the effects on young people of a late or missed visit. Again it seemed an instance where young people felt powerless to alter the behaviour of adults.

Summary

Clients' perceptions of care processes have been characterized in this chapter as the parents' disillusionment and the young people's sense of subjection to arbitrary authority. Although both reactions were provoked by the experience of care, it seems that their nature relates primarily to parents' and young people's attitudes and expectations *prior to care*. Parents were expecting something which residential care did not, in their eyes, provide, and it reinforced young people's sense of powerlessness and alienation, of being subject to arbitrary authority. In both cases, the historical context of the clients' views provided in our opinion a more effective means to understanding than the consideration of such variables as entry route, legal status, or type of placement. This is not to say that these factors are unimportant: in this chapter we have indicated how the existence of a care order changes the way a parent may withdraw moral sanction, and this issue will be taken further in the next chapter. But these variables seem to us to be of secondary importance in shaping clients' experiences.

The second principal theme of this chapter has been the lack of cohesiveness in the provision of field and residential social work as complementary resources. The lack of understanding of each other's role, the lack of communication, the use of residential care as a 'last resort' and difficulties updating philosophies of care, seem to have resulted in field and residential workers pulling against, more often than with, each other. As we have said in Chapters Three and Four, better pre-care negotiations and agreed clarity of purpose are prerequisites to improving the service. But a more radical approach is needed to establish a system of provision in which the arms of fieldwork and residential work belong to the same body.

6

Leaving care

Introduction

'Leaving care' is an ambiguous phrase because of the fact that 'in care' is both a legal state and a physical location. Sometimes leaving care means leaving in both the legal and physical sense, while at other times children physically leave care to go home but remain legally in the care of the local authority (a state referred to in this study as Trial Own Parent).

This chapter explores what leaving care meant to families and to their social workers. How did they negotiate for care to end? What brought them to this stage and what were the consequences for them? What actions were necessary and what, in hindsight, were parents' and childrens' views of care after it had ended?

The basis of the leaving care decision for the families

It was noted earlier that families with young people on care orders were under different constraints concerning the ending of care; for example dealing with a social worker alone was practically and emotionally different from dealing with a court. Families involved with the courts still felt they had a role in the decision to leave care, but they were more clearly aware of the existence of rules and formal processes. So in different ways, all the families felt that decision-making about leaving care involved them. They often put forward strong views about why care should end.

In making their decision, families had to balance the advantages and disadvantages of continuing care versus ending it. What tipped the balance in favour of ending care was either when the consequences (usually of return home) were perceived as trouble-free or when care itself was perceived as damaging and no longer acceptable. Families' decisions were, however, dominated by an assessment of the quality of care itself. As we have shown in earlier chapters, families had a standard for the acceptability or otherwise of care, and this was of paramount importance in shaping their perceptions of the processes of care. Ending care thus became important either because it was necessary to protect the young person from the effects of care, or because care at home now offered advantages.

It was unusual for parents and children to differ on the factors influencing their decision to end care: in only two cases were there instances of children emphasizing the disadvantages of care, while parents simply saw the advantages of leaving.

The families interviewed after the end of care therefore fell into two groups. One had made the judgement that care was acceptable but the alternative was better. The other simply assessed care as unacceptable. The leaving care decision was based on one of these two views. The judgement that care was unacceptable involved an assessment of the parenting standards of the care regime. As we shall see, this principally concerned appropriate control of the young person's behaviour (e.g. politeness to adults, limits on free choice, knowledge of whereabouts) which was also seen as a direct reflection of a genuine interest, or the lack of it, in the child.

Better alternatives

Families came to the view that there was a better alternative to care, as a result of changes in both parents and children. Parents' changes could involve the removal or addition of family members as well as changes in behaviour. To the children the changes in their own behaviour represented a process of maturing, while to their parents, they sometimes were seen as arising from the shock of the threat of removal from home having been made real.

> Mother: As soon as they'd gone I wanted them sort of back straightaway but I knew it were best for them, so that's why I left them where they were for the time being . . . [after six months] . . . I sorted myself out and I felt more relaxed. I had a boy-friend then . . . I just plucked a bit of courage up and spoke to him and he helped me over a lot of the difficult period . . . so with help from him I came to the conclusion that I think she were better off back home.

These comparative judgements were similar to those that the parents recalled making when they requested care in the first place. Listen, for example, to the same mother describing how her children came to be in care:

> I were getting very, very down and I didn't seem as though I wanted to bother about anything and I thought it would be the best thing for Susan and

the other two to have somebody else to take care of them for a while while I got myself sorted out. With my husband going sort of thing, it seemed as though all the world were coming down on me and I just couldn't seem to be able to manage it myself.

These judgements were not confined to voluntary requests for care.

> Mother: [The care order] was basically because of the trouble they'd got into. I sort of asked for . . . it . . . really, but I think the courts would have done it anyway because they just wouldn't stay out of trouble basically . . . both [my husband and I] had just about enough and I thought it would be the best thing for them . . . the environment had a lot to do with it because Bill and I, we were both working part-time night, the babysitter we had wasn't adequate and they just got into trouble . . . as soon as we got a place from the council you see, we got them back. Once we'd moved away from there and they'd done pretty well actually in care, so that was it.

The majority of parents had thought for various reasons that home life had become unacceptable and that care was needed. Over a period of time they revised the judgement about home, ending with a definite decision to have their children back. But for some families this parental change was less important than changes in the young persons themselves, which made alternatives to care seem the better option.

> Young person: I thought it were right clever being in homes and all this . . . but you see I think I were only about 14 [then] . . . [and after a while] I wanted to come home.

> Young person: . . . and then I started settling down after a bit and my dad died last year and that were a bit of a shock to me . . . and I settled down . . . so then I could show people that I can behave . . . I wanted to leave.

In some cases the changes in the young person may be regarded as just the usual process of growing up and maturing. One young person, nearing her seventeenth birthday in care, described leaving residential care to move to a flat with a boyfriend:

> I practically had to fight my way out. Because what they were doing, they were saying well, we'd better start thinking about it, and knowing that I was going I wanted to go. Not that I'm ungrateful for what they've done but I just felt I wanted to be free, I wanted to be me, I still don't know who me is, but I wanted to be me.

The decision that there was a better alternative reflected changing circumstances and changing views. For some parents this was related to the difficulties they had in coping and to the resolution of them; for some young people it was related to maturity, or to family changes influencing views of alternatives to care.

Unacceptable care

For the small group of families who came to the conclusion that care was unacceptable, the process of disillusion was typically rapid. For young people it sometimes followed a reasonable period in care, but for parents it always took place at the start of care, when they first found themselves learning in participative detail about residential parenting.

When the young people came to view care as unacceptable it was usually around the time in their life when they were starting to question rules and authority. One young man described his decision to leave (private) foster care as follows:

> It started off with there's a man that I've known all my life and I were going up to see him and [the foster parents] didn't want me to go and see him and I were a bit angry about this, and then one day I went up and it just broke out into an argument because I'd been. [My foster father] said that he were going to bounce me off all walls sort of thing and I think I got a bit mad about that and I said that I were leaving . . .

As the young people grew up they experienced previously acceptable or enforceable rules as unacceptable or unenforceable. But growing up also brought the need to start to make your own way in the world.

> Young person: I went down to Army Careers place and got some details and they said if I wanted to get in I'd have to be off a care order for at least six months, so I asked [my social worker] to put it through.

The fact that young people had started to find care unacceptable did not mean that their parents necessarily shared this view. Some young people acted independently of their parents in trying to get their views accepted, and in some cases, as we shall see, they effectively forced their parents to share their view that care was no longer acceptable and should end. For young people without parents there was not, of course, this possibility. One young man, received into care at an early age and with no contact with his parents, grew up in residential care. He had eight moves in his last two years. He found care unacceptable because of the fact that he had some 'worries living in homes and no family life'.

On the other hand, for parents, the unacceptability of care arose either from their eventual acceptance of their offspring's views, or from their own notion of acceptable parenting standards. They made judgements on residential care based on their increasing knowledge of it arising from both planned contact and from their need to respond to specific incidents.

> Mother: [My daughter] went missing several times and she was only there a month, practically every time we went she was missing. She never went to school, they dropped her off at school gates and that was it, she disappeared then, never went into school . . . nobody knew where she was or what she was doing or anything.

> Mother: I heard [the kids] talking to [the staff] . . . no respect whatsoever. And what annoyed me more were because [the staff] accepted it. No discipline . . . they don't learn them to respect their elders.

> Mother: I mean they could please themselves more or less what they wanted to do.

Some parents saw this lack of appropriate rules as providing a poor influence for their children which led to unfortunate consequences.

> Mother: We had a lot of problems in that way, doing everything what he thought were clever what the boys at the home had been doing . . . running away in afternoon from school glue sniffing.

If care was seen as being below a certain standard then whatever the other options it simply ceased to be acceptable.

> Mother: There was no way that I could have left her there no matter how I felt. I mean I know that things were still going to be very difficult and it was still going to be hard for her and me to cope with one another, but there was no way I could leave her there. I didn't even know places like that existed.

Disillusionment with care therefore grew out of direct knowledge of care. If parents found care unacceptable, this would usually occur soon after entry; if children found it unacceptable, it would usually occur at a period in their teenage life when they were challenging authority and the imposition on them of particular rules and norms. For either group it would be a fairly rapid process of disillusion characterized by a final snapping point that led to a desire to end care.

The family reformed

Earlier chapters have shown that parents continued to feel a high level of responsibility for their children after entry into care. Their view of the changes following entry to care was very much a practical one focusing on issues of day-to-day living. They worried about their children and they missed them, but on the whole care was seen as one of the many changes that families sometimes had to cope with, rather than as a break in the family's life. The children usually echoed this view, regarding their parents as continuing to have responsibilities and involvement in their care, but the practical changes were much harder for them. Very little in their day-to-day lives continued to be the same after they entered care.

The experience of leaving care echoed much of the experience of entry. The day-to-day responsibilities changed, but the actual business of being a parent, of feeling like a parent, usually continued before, during and after care. The parents did not therefore think there were many major changes, above the practical ones, resulting from their children leaving care, except in terms of their ability to take parental responsibility more seriously.

> Mother: I feel more relaxed knowing that she's safe because when she used to go out from [the foster parents] . . . you never knew what's going to happen to her, whereas if she's here I know that she's going to come through that door and if she's not back for a certain time I'm out looking for her. I feel more relieved that way. I can't really answer for [my daughter]. We do talk but we've never really discussed how she's felt since she came back. I think she's a bit more cheekier.

In fact for most children going home also raises major issues of parenting responsibilities, the most significant one for those in residential care being the shift from many people being responsible to just one or two.

> Young person: [Being out of care means I now] only have two people looking after me instead of many – [it's] better.

> Young person: You've got different people looking after you every day, different members of staff.

The physical change of living environment ('sharing bedrooms like, and getting up in a morning', many young people coming in from school 'cheering you up' and being around for activities and so on) was, of course, part of this shift from many to few carers, that the young people experienced. But the major component of this for the young people was the change from a feeling that no-one could be really concerned about them, to a difficult-to-explain feeling that somebody was now concerned. One girl put it like this:

> When I were in [children's home] they used to tell me to do something and I wouldn't do it, just sat there watching telly and just [did] what I wanted to and I wouldn't do nothing for them because I felt as though it were my job to do things for my family, not for anybody else.

She compared this with the feelings she now had at home:

> It's funny really because when I'm late coming in here, I know, I can feel it that I'm going to get into trouble. But when I were in the children's home I'm not really bothered, I weren't really bothered about being late because I knew that I could answer them back.

Knowing about their whereabouts and enforcing the rules made the young people feel that genuine concern was involved. The fact that this concern came from their families was also of great importance to them.

For children in foster care the issue of responsibility was somewhat different. One girl, for example, talked about the difficulties that a foster parent might have in trying to be responsible.

> I couldn't sleep out without asking [my foster parent] and she had to ask [my social worker] and then he had to phone up and it had to go through all this. I didn't think that were right really because whereas [my foster mother] would know where I was, that's all right, but when she's got to go and ask social services and all them lot if I can stay out, it's a bit much, isn't it?

Changes in the rules of everyday life did not greatly worry young people, although pocket money was mentioned, and the twin issues of bedtime and being allowed out appeared as sources of continuing and often continuous family debate. One had summed up the practical side of his new life as : 'Same things every day, school, telly, bed.'

But for others the impact of moving to care had meant a major move across the city and they described loneliness, not knowing new areas, and losing friends. After they had left care the great majority of young people said that they had changed *all* their friends again. Some mentioned just one friend that they still stayed in touch with from the care period. Parents occasionally objected to this friend from care, seeing this young person as an example of the 'contamination' of their child (see Chapter Five). In fact the friend was more likely to have come from the pre-care period. The young person had stayed in touch with bad company, in the parents' eyes, for a number of years but now it could be directly associated with care. Interestingly, and uniquely, one young person who had gone to detention centre said that all his friends were made there, and he only had friends from there. The major friendship changes experienced by nearly all the young people probably reflect similar changes when families move area or children change schools; these young people experienced this phenomenon without the continuing care of familiar adults.

Only one or two young people said they had kept contact with care staff or foster parents, although one or two more hoped to do so.

For most of them coming back home enabled them to pick up again on the familiar practical things of their life, and this was viewed positively. The families who had children at home on care orders did not, of course, have practical changes to cope with once care ended. Indeed they regarded the ending of the care order as a total non-event. Most did not attend the court, and all of them, parents and children alike, commented that the only effect would be the end of the social worker's visiting. Even this was not seen as important because for the great majority social work visits were seen as purely routine, or just friendly.

Both parents and young people thought they were prepared in themselves for the changes that the move from care entailed; usually considering this in terms of their continuing sense of being a family, and then equating preparation with agreement or commitment to the move. Apart from valuing discussion about the move, one preparation issue was regularly raised by parents and children. Both thought that an agreement about rules, and how they were to be enforced, was an important issue in the changes that had taken place.

Young person: [There haven't been any difficulties about rules] because we talked them out before, just before I came and I agreed with them so I just stay by the rules.

Father: I made a promise to [the social worker] like, that I would sit in authority [and take responsibility].

Fieldworkers' views

Fieldworkers had rather less to say about ending care than their clients. We shall consider their views in contrast to the clients', and then look at the actions they saw themselves taking, and how, if at all, that involved other workers.

Fieldworkers' descriptions of the processes of ending care followed closely those given by the families; they universally agreed that family views had changed along one of the two dimensions that have been explored above. In terms of the actual events there was also very close agreement between the fieldworkers' and the families' accounts. This was true for cases even where major incidents had occurred when a fieldworker was ill, or on holiday at the time of ending care.

Changes in family perceptions about better alternatives, unacceptable care or periods of trouble-free behaviour were seen in similar ways by fieldworkers and families. However, the understanding of the basis of these changes was different in that the fieldworkers were more in tune with the young people's views than with the parents' views. They often understood quite clearly the ways that young people were changing during their time in care and the ways that young people came to re-assess the appropriateness of care for themselves.

> Fieldworker: I think he realized that the things that kids get up to in care, the reasons that they're put there, aren't so glamorous as perhaps he thought at one point . . . He's had to do some serious thinking about himself and his life . . . he's come out more mature, more stable and thoughtful than he was before . . . I should imagine he sometimes misses a bit of the excitement that can happen in a children's home and getting into scrapes with his peer groups.

> Fieldworker: It was no good people telling [the young person] that what he was doing was bad for him and all the rest of it because it didn't register . . . it had to come from him . . . as he got older he began to accept that what people tell him and had been telling him all these years wasn't so much hogwash. . . . I think it's basically a process of maturing.

Most social workers were not nearly as perceptive about the feelings of parents, offering in their accounts very little analysis of the basis of the parents' view or understanding of the ways that parents would see the children's return home. The main differences between parents and social workers therefore lay in the absence from most social workers' accounts of any discussion of continuing parental responsibility, and how that was to be practically enacted when a child returned home. However, a small number of social workers did pick up this issue, to both parents' and children's satisfaction, and we shall return to them later in this chapter.

Social workers all said that they had discussed leaving care with various family members. In some cases, this involved discussions *after* the decision and event had taken place. One family, for example, moved their daughter home when a social worker was on holiday; in another case a young person pressed his mother to take him back, and the social worker was informed only after this had happened. Sometimes these actions were taken by residential staff; we have one account of staff deciding that a young person must leave, offering his mother the choice of either returning home or removal elsewhere in the country, and then arranging discharge to home without involving the field social worker at any stage. Most social workers did, of course, know about the discharge in advance, but a good number of discharge processes (according to both families and social workers), occurred without the *active involvement* of the social worker.

The care order cases (needing court action for discharge) did, of course, have the direct involvement of the social worker. The social workers agreed with the families' view that discharge was appropriate after a period of trouble-free behaviour. There were various yardsticks applied to the definition of this period.

> Social worker: I could have gone for revocation at least six months before, but I held back and he knew that the slightest offence . . . so that you didn't make an idiot of yourself and the boy in court, he's got to be blemish-free.

> Social worker: Mum had always asked for discharge, right from way back, and I said, well, I've given her vague time limits in the past, saying, well, if in a year or so or if in two years, what have you, and [then] I was saying we'll do it within the near future and then I got on with it.

There did not appear to be a great deal of agreement between social workers about the length of this trouble-free period, nor was there always much clarity about its definition. Some social workers discussed this period as if it were a form of supervised suspended sentence, while others conceptualized it much more loosely, operating on the general idea that if there was no trouble then one day they would return to court.

Social workers did not have much to say about their actions and roles in the child's leaving care except in terms of general discussions with families and, where appropriate, a supervisory function. They usually had a clear view of the events surrounding leaving care, but a less clear view of their role within that. A few social workers did, however, see their role in terms of organizing an agreement about return home (or movement to another placement) and taking actions to enact that agreement. The main actions that they discussed were those of trying to organize some of the elements of the new placement, and helping the child with the details of the move itself. Social workers in these cases were those who showed the greater awareness in their accounts of the issues concerning responsibility discussed above, and this was the main issue that they concentrated on when they were organizing the new setting. Remember, for example, the father quoted earlier.

> I made a promisee to [the social worker] like, I would sit in authority [and take responsibility].

Social workers put this emphasis on continuing responsibility in the following way:

> [Coming into care] was done on a written contract basis. During the interval they were in care, mother made certain agreements to do decorating and do various things and it was agreed that her daughter would come out of care just before the new baby was going to be born.

Another social worker:

> We have drawn up contracts about her going out and what time she should come back, that she should have spending money of her own and there should be some agreement as to what it is spent on.

Whereas factual matters relating to leaving care were almost always shared, it was exceptional for social workers to have knowledge of the families' views of such issues as continuing responsibility or the re-introduction of parental authority. When social workers did have such knowledge, they were more actively involved in decisions to end care. In the majority of cases, however, the business of leaving care was a more shadowy event for the social workers than for the families, who saw their workers as rather shadowy themselves.

At the point of entry to care families had seen their social workers as powerful controllers of agency resources. The experience of practitioners was quite different as they saw themselves as relatively powerless, even though individually responsible, within their agency. They described, for example, the way that other staff controlled access to residential care, and how the range of resources (not necessarily the quantity) greatly constrained choice. When care was under way this powerless but responsible feeling was felt even more acutely by residential staff. The practitioners therefore saw themselves as subject to the systems around them rather than as part of a team serving clients. By the time care ended, the sense of individual isolation of most practitioners had continued to develop. The involvement of other staff, for example, was very rarely mentioned as part of the leaving care process. One or two described the impact of a community scheme or a new teacher on the development of the young person: but there was no reference to any active collaboration over the young person leaving care. As regards social services staff, only two social workers specifically mentioned any involvement of residential workers or foster parents. They had somewhat different experiences to recount:

[Discharge] had always been the plan between myself and the residential staff.

I talked about it with the staff at [the children's home], but things tended to happen in two separate ways, I mean what [the children's home] were saying to her wasn't the same thing they'd been saying to me, so in the end I was sort of taking things from what the teenager was saying rather than from anyone else.

All the social workers predominantly saw themselves as working very much on their own, although in just under half the cases they mentioned some involvement with headquarters staff; namely, Principal Social Workers (Team Leaders) and the court section. According to the social workers, all the other cases were handled entirely on their own. The pattern of headquarters consultation was directly related to the legal category of the case. None of the social workers involved in voluntary cases said that they had consulted any other agency staff when working on the process of discharge from care. On the other hand, with the care order cases, most had been discussed with the court section, and half had been discussed with the Principal Social Worker. The court section would be directly involved if court actions were contemplated. As one social worker put it:

It would be standard procedure I think on anything which would involve things to do with care orders.

Ending care, unlike the rest of care, did not have agency systems that made practitioners involve other staff except for the court appearances. Given the choice about this involvement practitioners worked on their own, and there was very little evidence of social workers acting as part of a team, or of collaborating with various individuals (other than clients) to arrange discharge from care. They saw their practice as needing to rely heavily on their own initiatives, and they saw themselves within the agency as individually responsible workers.

The actions taken to leave care

Given the views which have just been outlined, what actions did families take to bring about the end of care?

The principal actions families took involved: requests to social workers to end care, briefing a solicitor, attendance at court (although not active involvement in court), and the simple collection of their child. Around half of the families said that their actions had been discussed with their social workers. Families said that social workers 'knew' of these actions, and many commented that they 'agreed with them' about them; so, in general, they were clear that discussions had taken place. There were, however, only a few families who expressed the view that their discussions involved any joint planning of actions. The common view was of actions being agreed with, rather than planned with, their social worker. A small minority of families described actions to leave care taken in conjunction with their social worker. We shall return to this minority later in this chapter.

Other families described very different processes. Some saw their actions as being quite independent of their social workers. For instance, some young people took actions to convince others that they no longer needed care. These young people told us that they decided 'to settle down', or 'fight their way out' or to 'keep out of trouble'. Sometimes they simply presented their social worker with a fait accompli.

> I asked [my mum] if I could come back. I didn't leave on spur of moment, I left it about a week ., . . [after I left] I saw [my social worker] once and she asked questions and then she said as long as things were all right at home, it's all right.

On occasions parents did the same.

> Mother: My husband and I talked it over and we both agreed that if she was going to come home eventually, it was better to fetch her just there and then . . . I just went to [reception centre] . . . and I just simply stated in front of one of the workers or whoever it is that works there looks after them, look, if you're coming home, if you want to come home, you'd better be at my house for lunchtime tomorrow.

A small number of families therefore described their action as being quite independent of any discussions that they may have had with social workers about leaving.

Another group of families felt that they had very little involvement in the process at all. Some of this group had felt unconcerned about care ending because of the lack of impact, as they saw it, of a care order when the child was at home. For these families care just lapsed when the young person concerned reached 18. But for two families the lack of involvement was rather different, and they described the process of ending care as something that professionals did with minimal family involvement.

Mother: The social worker said that she finds that my daughter is keeping out of trouble, and [is] getting on fine, so she could take her off the care order and I accepted that.

One mother described a bewildering process:

. . . all of a sudden social worker come and said that you can have her home or they'll send her to . . . is it a remand centre or somewhere, they'd send her somewhere, but you could have her home, just like that and I can't understand it to this day why.

This is her daughter, describing the same event:

It were about half an hour before I came home they told me I'd got to put my stuff and that . . . [the children's home] phoned my mum and dad and then half an hour after that they told me to go home and I'd got half an hour to pack all my stuff and staff were just chucking stuff in bags.

The social workers' *accounts* of the actions taken to leave care agreed with their clients' accounts, with the only noticeable difference in those cases where there had been consultation by social workers with other agency staff (i.e. care order cases). As in entry to care, clients did not appear to know of this consultation. The number of decision-makers would typically increase when asking children, parents and social workers. So it was seen, for example as 'mum' by the young person, 'social worker and me' by mum, and 'social worker, principal social worker, court section, mum and young person' by the social worker.

Looking back on it

After the end of care both parents and children provided views on the changes that had occurred during the care period, and the ways that they had presented that period to other people. They also discussed changes that had occurred during the care period.

From the parents' point of view the major effect of care was a noticeable change in the behaviour of their children. They thought their children showed an increased appreciation of life at home. Mothers' typical comments were:

I'm hoping it's changed his attitude towards me and made him appreciate me a bit more.

I think it did make her appreciate home a little bit more.

I think she might appreciate me a bit better.

Occasionally this was linked to dislike of care. One father, for example, commented:

> I think in the long run [care] must have done her good because she definitely didn't like it there.

Only two parents also told us that care had sometimes affected their children in worrying ways. As one mother commented:

> It's left its mark on her. You've got to keep ensuring her that she's wanted all the time, you've got to keep telling her you love her all the time.

Most of the parents in our study thought that care had made their children value their home more; just two voiced concern about the effect of the period on their children's emotional development.

The young people saw changes in themselves as well. As we have seen earlier, their friendships changed dramatically, but the major personal change for most of the children was that the experience had brought them closer to their family. They thought of their family, they sometimes missed it, and they started to feel different about it. They described themselves as 'growing up' and 'maturing' while in care, while 'learning to accept a bit more rules which I couldn't before'. A few described care as making them more thoughtful about themselves and their life. Listen to this 18 year old for example:

> When I was younger I used to look down on poor people, then I used to think god, the least they could do is be clean and have nice clothes, but you just can't, that's the way they are and you've got to take them and they are a person inside, there's good in them somewhere. . . . You'd have hated me before because I was so arrogant . . . [care's] made me . . . talk freely about me, all my bad points, and I can take criticism too. Some people go off, 'Well, I'm not like that', but if you tell something about me I'll try and do something about it.

This developing thoughtfulness was not always valued by parents. Listen, for example, to the mother of a different girl:

> It's changed her character. She never used to sit and think a lot like she does now. She were a right happy child, she could take things easier, but now she doesn't.

These changes in behaviour resembled the 'more humble' attitudes the parents discussed as part of their hopes for care – humility which took the form of appreciation of home, and of accepting rules.

Some parents expressed anxiety about the effects of the care period on themselves:

Mother: I've got that insecure feeling still. It doesn't matter how long they're back with you . . . I've seemed to have thought, oh, everything's going smooth and then all of a sudden it's started up again and he's took off. It really hurts you . . . I always thought I knew my kids properly and the way they turned out I couldn't understand it because to me I'd done best I thought possible for them but in some ways I lack somewhere, failed them somewhere.

These were parents whose teenage children had played a major role in the admission to care, a role that had left its mark on the parents at the time.

Mother: I think he wanted care . . . I were a bit heartbroken when I took him in like.

For these families alone care had apparently led to a questioning of their ability as parents, which lasted beyond the initial entry and beyond any subsequent discussions or changes. They felt unsure about their capacity to understand their child, and anxious about the same breakdown occurring again. Families where care arose from criminal charges, care proceedings, or parental requests did not mention this continuing unease; it was mentioned only in cases where children had, in their parents' eyes, made a judgement about care and found the family wanting in some respect. None of the social workers involved mentioned this parental unease, and neither they nor the young people reported any post-care discussions about the child's initial judgement of the family. In other respects the accounts of the social workers echoed those of the families, but with greater knowledge being shown of the young people's views.

How had parents and children presented care to others?

The only parents who voiced any concern about presenting the care episode to other people were those whose children were subject to criminal care orders (S.7(7)).

Mother: At the time they blamed, as if it was me that had him put away and it were terrible. I mean it's parents that take it every time.

Mother: We were upset because he was away, we were both upset, we didn't like it at all and it was something that I didn't mention to anybody, in fact I didn't want anybody to find out because I was ashamed to think that a son of mine could have got into trouble like that and had to be put away.

The shame and the resulting secrecy led to rumours and further problems.

109

Mother: Even a friend of mine I didn't tell until one day she mentioned it that her lad, he went to the same school as my son . . . had said, oh, do you know Mrs So-and-so's lad, they've told me that he's been sent to Borstal, and of course I told her then. She said why didn't you tell me before, she says I've got three lads myself, I said because I was ashamed.

For the other families there was much less concern. They thought that the problems in their family had been prominently visible for a long time to good friends and to schools. So the need to explain was minimal, and there was little difficulty in doing so if required. There were, however, clear boundaries on the number of people they would want their business known to; these did not stretch beyond close family friends, schools and other involved social agencies.

Mother: The friends that we've got we've had for years and they know the problems anyway. They were a bit surprised I think when I finally did put her into a foster home. They weren't surprised when I brought her out funnily enough . . . [the school] knew the problems well in advance.

Father: Most [of our friends] know the problems from start to finish.

The social workers were not sure what the families' attitude to presenting care had been, and they gave no indication of having discussed this topic.

The children had in general more worries than their parents, (although none of the children on S.7(7) care orders described feelings of shame). They were usually reluctant to discuss personal family issues with their peers.

I don't tell them why because it's nothing to do with nobody else so I just don't tell them why . . . I just say that I've been in care and that I'm back, so that's it.

I just say my family's split up, that's about all.

They found this rather more difficult when they needed to describe what care had been like.

They ask what it's like and things like that, I said they wouldn't like to be in care because they'd miss their family and that, but it's just something that comes natural isn't it, if you've got to go in care you have to go in care.

There were problems with stereotyped views:

The more mature people tend to understand, but there are two younger girls, my age group, that I'm working with and I don't think they know what care really is, and it were like at school that girl who said 'bars on the window' . . . I say it's not like a prison or anything like that, it's just like a big house.

So the young people did have some difficulties in describing why they were in care and what care was like, but only a small minority of social workers showed any knowledge of this.

Social work action and the quality of care

Most of the parents and children involved in our study looked back on care with some positive views. Even those parents who described to us their eventual view of care as unacceptable, nonetheless commented on some positive effects on their child's behaviour; their child had, they thought, learnt that other options were no better and were sometimes worse than their own home. On the other hand, the group of parents who found care acceptable also had a contrasting side to their views, outlining some bad effects on themselves or their children. Different elements of care were evaluated on different bases by the different participants.

Within this overall picture there were, however, just a few families who were outstandingly positive about their field social worker. These positive views were associated with clear statements of satisfaction about care, despite the fact that admission had sometimes been a desperate step for them. There was nothing about care that distinguished this little group of four families from all the others. Voluntary cases and S.1(2) and S.7(7) care orders were all represented, and the children had been in residential and foster care for varying periods at varying ages.

The positive views held about the social workers were expressed very forcefully:

Mother: I think if it weren't for him I think I would have done something really drastic to start with. I'd have probably ended up killing myself or trying to anyway if it hadn't been for him.

Mother: I've had lots of social workers [over the past 20 years] . . . and there were only one other one that was as good as her . . . she's a smashing lass [my social worker] is meant for that job.

Young person: She's not my social worker, she's my friend . . . in fact she's more than a friend she's someone special.

These cases were notable for the convergence of social worker and family understanding of the family's situation: the social worker could describe the family's views in similar ways to the family's own descriptions, and the families were better able to describe the role of the social worker, commenting on his or her openness and reliability of approach.

This group of families formed an interesting minority. Social workers did appreciate these parents' views about the continuing responsibility during care. They also expressed an understanding of the importance of presenting the care episode to others for some parents and some children. It was also noted earlier that most social workers were less aware of the parents' views than they were of the young people's. This was not true for this minority; they appeared to the children and to the parents as people who took them seriously, and were able to describe views of events that were congruent with those of adults and children.

It was equally the case that these families understood the workers more clearly in terms of both role and approach. Recollection of worker actions and the purpose of actions was clearer. As has been mentioned before, the use of contracts and agreements was one aspect of this, but so was the idea that options were put to the family, and then suitably discussed and agreed. For example, these are mothers' recollections of the start of care:

> Yes, well, me and [my social worker] talked about it and he said he thought it were a good idea but it'd have to be me that decided, he wasn't going to take them off me, so I said I thought it were a good idea, get myself sorted out. I had to really think about it, he gave me plenty of time and I thought it were best for kids.

> [My social worker] had suggested [care], that it might be a possibility, but he didn't force the issue at all, it was my sort of say so eventually they did go into care.

The parents also valued the reliability and honesty of these social workers and the fact that they put their cards on the table. They thought that the social workers had always done what had been agreed, and that agreement had always involved them. As one mother put it:

> He never went behind my back and did something without telling me, he'd ask or come and discuss it.

These families were the *only* ones who mentioned the possibility of returning for more help if they had problems in the future, and they said they would recommend others to do the same. This was unique to this group; a group who had found their social workers honest and purposeful, and also found them willing to accept that the parents' and children's point of view was to be taken very seriously indeed. They had often been reluctant clients to begin with, but they ended up valuing social services very highly.

> Mother: [This care period has] made me appreciate my life a lot more and also that no matter how far down you get, if you can go to the right places you get help, even if it's just talking, you can get help. I would advise anybody that were in similar situation as I've been in not to let themselves get that far down but just turn to social services, because I used to think they were right ogres, right bad guys and you only went there if you were really going to commit suicide or something like that, but I found out different, you don't have to.

Summary

The clients' views outlined in this chapter have been shaped by direct knowledge of the *complete* care process. With this knowledge, and with a focus on leaving care, they have echoed many of the themes that have been introduced in earlier chapters. They have described, in various ways, their continuing sense of being a family, throughout the care period, and some of the issues that were involved. They have discussed the way they sanctioned care in the context of a decision to end it. The changes generated by a move of home have been outlined, and the changes that occurred during care have been touched on. With the return home, or the move to independent living, the parents and their children have faced new problems as well as ones featured in earlier stages of care, such as discipline and rules.

The overall view emerging from the families' accounts is that leaving care is part of an evolutionary process. Views change, action is taken, the new situation is coped with and stabilized. There were antecedents to leaving care just as for entry. There were new social relationships to form for children and for adults, just as there had been in care (e.g. friends, peers, neighbours, schools, social agencies, and the family itself). Problems that led to care, and new problems, needed to be dealt with before the family was stabilized in its new form. Families saw and dealt with all these issues for better or for worse. Field social workers, on the other hand, gave a much more limited account of ending care. The great majority focused on the middle period of leaving care: the practical business of leaving physical care and moving, or the court business of leaving legal care. The importance of arranging the move in service terms (administration, organization of payments, notifications, etc.), the necessity to fulfil the legal requirements, and the fact that the most obvious event in leaving care is often the legal or physical move, may have concentrated social workers' attentions: theirs was a much narrower set of concerns than those identified by families.

In essence, most social workers described ending care as an event, while most families described it as a process. Of course, for families ending care, the transfer of responsibility was usually a matter of degree rather than a clear-cut demarcation. Social workers did not usually sense the continuing responsibility felt within families. In fact the parents were often rather unknown quantities, and the social worker would typically know more about the changes and developments in the children rather than changes in the family as a whole. Most social workers appeared to focus on the young person in care, with the family reappearing, as it were, when care was ending. On the other hand, the views of a small number of parents and young people concerning the quality of care were significantly more positive when social workers had stayed in close touch with parents as well as children, and when they had acted in a way described as 'open and honest'.

In general, the process of ending care was not accorded much attention by most social workers. On the whole, their accounts of ending care were much less detailed than their accounts of entry to care. They gave little emphasis to their actions to end care, and this view was shared by their clients. For social workers entry to care was typically rapid and involved a great deal of activity, while ending care was usually just the reverse.

7

Rethinking child care policy

The raising of children is an intensely private family matter which is nevertheless the subject of equally intensive public debate and concern. We have all been children, some of us are parents, and we all in various ways take responsibility for children. We are all curious to know what really goes on in other families and all equally determined to preserve the privacy of our own family life. Despite this interest in the way families raise their children, there nevertheless remains a fundamental belief that parents have an inviolable right to determine their children's upbringing independently of outside interference. This is the context of the experiences described in the previous chapters. The families and the professionals have been concerned with the care of children and with negotiating the criteria that govern state intervention in that care.

Changing families and changing policy

The public system of child care in the UK has been dominated by the twin themes of rescue and compensation. The law has long recognized the right of society to remove children from parents who are believed to be damaging them and, in recent times, has become alert to more subtle kinds of damage. This judicial readiness to sanction rescue was revised in post-war years in the light of Bowlby's work on maternal deprivation. However, the effect of Bowlby's studies has been contradictory. In one sense, he re-emphasized the sanctity of the maternal relationship and its centrality to psychological health. This served to raise the rescue threshold by warning of the possible damage to the child of removal from the family. In another sense, however, the research could be interpreted as pointing to the necessity to ensure that, once crossed, the threshold of removal should lead to a particular, compensatory form of care in recognition of the child's maternal loss. These themes are alive and well in British child care policy at both a national and a local level.

These psychological principles which once guided thinking about the planning of child care services are, of course, founded on particular notions about the composition of 'normal' families and about the nature of family relationships. The child's alleged psychological need for unbroken maternal presence fits neatly with dominant conceptions of 'proper' family life, in which the mother's role in upbringing far outweighs that of the father. Such a view of family life coincided in the UK with an intense concentration during the fifties on the mother as the primary guarantor of children's health and welfare (Oakley, 1981; Wilson, 1977) and aligns comfortably with the period's economic boom and reconstructionist philosophy.

These are, however, highly questionable principles in the moral and practical minefield of child care policy. The decision about whether and when to intervene in unhappy families cannot be resolved simply by reference to psychological theories, nor can it be based on folk precepts about not interfering. When to intervene, who should be given powers to do so, and with what long-term aims, are questions which challenge our fundamental social organization and values.

Moreover, these traditional wisdoms of family life do not survive modern scrutiny. In the first place, the very composition of families is changing. The pattern of permanent two-parent, two-children families has shifted, and the boundaries of family membership are now more fluid (see Rapoport et al, 1982). It is becoming more common for families to consist of a series of parent figures in various relationships to a series of children. As is so often the case, the evolving terminology used to describe families epitomizes these changes. When the family norm was permanence, the term 'broken family', with its aura of irretrievable loss and disgrace, was used. A current term, 'reconstituted families' (Burgoyne and Clarke, 1982), describing families where a new parent figure is incorporated, neatly encapsulates the concept of an evolving family unit whose nature is changed, rather than destroyed, by the arrivals and departures of various members.

Related changes have also occurred in the nature of parenting itself. The concept of the father's and the mother's discrete and unconnected contributions to the psychological and physical well-being of the child is less tenacious in modern child psychology. The 'discovery' of the role of the father in child development, in particular his ability to achieve significant interaction with the child despite the apparent handicap of significantly less time to do so (see, for example, Lamb 1981), has led to a revision of the basic tenets of parenting. So too has the rise of feminist versions of the nature of parenting, in which, for example, the daily physical care of children has been demystified to lay bare the sheer labour involved, and hence the need to share this burden equally rather than regard it as an unequivocal privilege (see, for example, Oakley, 1974).

Increasingly parents regard their contributions as interchangeable and allocate parental roles on the basis of competence, availability and equality and not simply gender. These changes have considerable implications for the criteria for social work intervention in the lives of families and for the nature of public child care provision.

Political dimensions of child care policy

If these changes in family structure and parental roles are of recent origin, current political dimensions of child care policy, which have rarely been more prominent than today, surely have a longer history.

The tension between the rights of parents, of their children, and of the state, which attracted increasing legislative attention in the UK during the nineteenth century, continues to be demonstrated in the concerns of pressure groups in recent years. The increasing emphasis on the rights of children in the campaigns of Equality For Children and of Justice For Children are mirrored in increasing legislative concern for the child's wishes. Equally vociferous are the parent-oriented Campaign For One-Parent Families and the Family Rights Group, whose arguments for the rights of parents in the face of state intervention have contributed to the pressure which produced the recent DHSS Code of Practice relating to access to children in care. Thus the pendulum of public pressure swings back and forth, reflecting the unresolved tensions within public policy.

In political terms, the relationship between the family and the state has always included at its core both the right of the family to raise children as it sees fit, and the corresponding right of the state to intervene if the family's care or control falls short of what the state requires. Law and custom thus defend the family as the prime agent of socialization only in so far as it fulfils the task currently prescribed. The construction of this task is a dynamic process which varies from age to age and society to society.

A constant theme in this process has been the family's duty to take responsibility for its members, to inculcate socially acceptable behaviour, and to safeguard virtues in danger of erosion through either time or opposition. Thus hard work, education and moral tutelage are some of the guiding principles behind parent-child relationships, and much parental ingenuity and anxiety is expended in finding opportunities to introduce or reinforce these messages. However, in legitimating

117

these tasks, the legal framework established by the state has inevitably suffered from some confusion over whether it is primarily directed at helping families to achieve social control of their children or at ratifying state intervention.

The evolution of British law governing the moral and physical welfare of children exemplifies this confusion. Legal authority over children was vested in kin until the demand, engendered by the industrial revolution, for cheap factory labour from children (Alcock and Harris, 1982; Morris et al, 1980; Dingwall, Eekelaar and Murray, 1983) caused children to work outside the parent's sphere of authority, rendering children's behaviour and working circumstances a target for state as well as family control.

Thus the generation of the framework of British child welfare legislation never derived simply from the interests of the child; instead the dominant force was the need for social regulation. As Dingwall and his colleagues comment (1983):

> Attention was first focused on protection from children and only latterly on protection of children.

There is, in fact, a tension between legal concepts designed to facilitate state control over family life, and those designed to protect the family from undue state intervention and to boost family autonomy.

Nowhere is this tension better demonstrated than in the provision of the British system of social services. The particular relationship between the state and the family embodied in the system of public welfare gives rise to considerable concern over the extent to which such provisions boost or erode family autonomy. Family responsibility to care for its members has become shared with health and education authorities, social security and social services to a greater extent than ever before, and there has always been a concern that the welfare state may undermine family ties and produce welfare dependency. One political response to this has been to attempt to reinforce the role of the family as the primary carer, and to identify why some families appear throughout generations to be unable to solve their problems without recourse to public assistance.

The identification of family authority over children with the interests of the state is strongly aligned with the political view that the family should be encouraged to accept total responsibility for its members. Such a strong family unit has both emotional appeal, as underpinning moral virtues under current threat, and considerable economic appeal, as reducing the demand for costly public care of dependency groups.

This philosophy finds expression in some recent social thought and has been most notably promulgated in the area of social services, producing on the far right a philosophy of welfare in which the care of family members is increasingly seen as a private problem, to be undertaken using family resources only, and to be underpinned only in extreme circumstances by a residual network of statutory services.

In the UK (and the USA) this has been the recent drift of government programmes. In Britain, the Social Services Minister, Sir Keith Joseph, made the now famous speculations on the inadequacy of working-class parenting and the need for better 'preparation for parenthood'. The funds given by the DHSS under Sir Keith for research into the 'cycle of deprivation' were the practical expression of this policy. At the inception of this UK research programme designed to examine the inter-generational transmission of poverty, Harriet Wilson (1973) investigated the relevance of Sir Keith's ideas on 'preparation for parenthood' to resolving the problems of poor families in inner cities. She concluded that the research indicated the need, not for social training, but for:

> large-scale fiscal measures to speed up slum clearance and housing schemes, to improve local amenities, to boost family incomes by generous family allowances, to improve the job market in the inner city, and to implement the proposed extension of nursery provision.

Not surprisingly, the research commissioned by the DHSS failed to identify any attitudinal mechanism by which poverty was somehow 'transmitted' from parent to child. Instead, the studies pointed to a complex exchange between traditional attitudes and stark economic deprivation of the kind described by Wilson (see Blaxter and Paterson, 1982; Coffield, Robinson and Sarsby, 1982). Despite this, primary preventive measures of the sort recommended by Wilson have not emerged in public policy.

Furthermore, the fear that the welfare state is undermining family responsibility is unfounded (Longfield, 1984). Policy changes are being pressed on the basis of myths. British studies of family life and family preferences for care for dependents indicate that family members have essentially retained their primary caring role, and prefer care in *partnership* with public agencies rather than wishing to hand it over (see Moroney, 1976; West, 1984).

The child care legacy

In relation to child care policy, this fear of undermining responsibility results from a fundamental misunderstanding of the role of parents, and reinforces the antipathy between public and private care of children. As other commentators have noted (Millham et al, 1984), the history of social policy in this field has bequeathed a legacy of disregard for the potential of the family as a continuing source of security for children identified in some way as being at risk.

This disregard of the family's potential for constructive future contact where the question of the adequacy of a child's parenting has arisen, has led to a polarization of public care and private family life. Public care is seen as inevitably damaging the psychological health of the child and as a verdict on the parents' abilities to offer appropriate care. By contrast, the family remains the haven of proper child development. The evidence presented earlier indicating that there are many different patterns of family composition, and that caring is frequently shared with others than the direct family, changes radically our conceptions of what help is relevant when parents find child care difficulties beyond their solution.

Clearly the very notion that responsibility for child development is best shared among a range of people, with stimuli for education and play, attention for health matters and so on deliberately shared between parents and professionals, has immediate implications for the public response when families encounter difficulties in child care. Add to this the notion that in very many families, as a matter of daily routine, the simple care of children (other than for educational or health purposes) is entrusted to minders, friends and wider family, and it is clear that there is no such thing as the exclusive care of children by their parents. All parenting is shared between the family and the wider kinship and friendship network, and between this system and state provision.

The consequence of this is that public services designed to develop the potential of children and to safeguard their health and welfare must aim for an approach which incorporates the concept of *partnership* at its core, and that the legal framework relating to intervention in families should recognize and encourage this sense of partnership. In some services, this recognition already exists, at least in a rudimentary form. Few dispute that the health of children is primarily the responsibility of the parents, and much intervention is designed to educate parents in the physical care of their children. Nursing and medical intervention is therefore dependent on parental notification, and subsequent care, particularly in relation to young children, can often be exercised only through the parents. However imperfectly practised, this approach at least recognizes that health care intervention must supplement that of the parents rather than substitute for it. It is this emphasis on *supplementary* rather than *substitute* care (Davis, 1981), growing out of a recognition of the fundamentally shared nature of parenting, which should be the driving force behind a new direction for child care policy.

Collaboration or compulsion?

It is, of course, nothing new to propose that the legal framework of child welfare and professional intervention should reflect the need to work with, rather than against, families. As the government circular explaining the 1948 Children Act put it (Circular 48/160):

> To keep the family together must be the first aim, and the separation of the child from its parents can only be justified when there is no possibility of securing adequate care for that child in his own home.

Much of the legislation governing public intervention in family life is in fact concerned with laying a duty on public authorities to 'diminish the need to receive children into or keep them in care' (Child Care Act 1980, S.1), while the terminology of the law emphasizes the *reception* of children into care, rather than the popular phrase 'taking them into care'. This is not mere semantics. Public authorities have extensive discretion in their operation of the law relating to child welfare (Alcock and Harris, 1982), and are legally empowered to offer a preventive service aimed at supporting families in their caring for children. The popular image of the 'welfare' removing children, however well it may reflect the service given by social services in the eyes of its recipients and of ratepayers, is only a pale reflection of the legal obligations on public authorities. As with every area of social welfare, practical intervention and the legal authority for it may be worlds apart in their nature and effects, as we have seen in a number of different aspects of this research study.

The potential emphasis in the legislative framework on permissive intervention, implying the co-operation of families in ensuring the adequate care of their childrem, relates primarily to services designed to prevent the need for admission to care. In its practical implementation by public authorities, the legislative framework may well give some scope for recognizing the potential of family care *prior* to care. When admission has taken place, however, the legacy of public and professional attitudes towards parents whose children have entered public care often appears an insurmountable obstacle to any further constructive contact between parents and their children.

121

The aura of compulsion in the public child care services has been extensively analysed in recent years. Parton (1979 and 1981) and Packman (1981) both highlight an apparently increasing tendency for intervention in family life to be based on compulsion rather than informal permission, and attribute this either to defensive practice in the context of possible exposure (Packman), or to the fact that social work practice is merely reflecting a change in the moral climate of society towards greater social control of deviance (Parton). As this is being written (in 1985), the publicity given to the case of Jasmine Beckford, who died after she was returned from public care to her parents' care, will ensure that social workers will once again be reminded of the need to respond to the apparently contradictory demands of society both to intervene effectively and to respect family autonomy.

These theories regarding the increasing use of compulsion have been criticized by Dingwall and his colleagues (1983), as lacking in authoritative statistical basis, and lacking any overview of the *relative*, as opposed to *absolute*, use of compulsory intervention. According to these critics, the use of compulsory powers to protect children is, in fact, declining in relation to the number of children who may require such protection.

Although the question whether there is any way of determining those in need of protection is at the heart of this debate, this is unlikely to be the prime determinant of professional practice. It seems clear that, no matter how those at risk may be identified and quantified, social workers will, in practice, increasingly want to ensure that their actions are directed by legislative requirements, both as protection for themselves and as a means of pointing to at least some external criteria for the validity of the protective actions taken in respect of children. Thus there seems a prima facie risk that social work intervention will increasingly be characterized by recourse to legal justification, and that, regardless of the debate about whether compulsion is on the increase, the public care of children will be further identified with compulsory removal and thus as antipathetic to family care. The findings from this study point to an alternative way forward.

The clients' contribution

This danger calls increasing attention to a second issue, namely how such intervention is experienced by families. The analysis of the effects of social policy by interpreting official statistics remains the favourite method of social commentators, despite now extensive evidence that such an approach relies on social indicators which are at best artificially constructed and at worst downright misleading. In the area of child care policy, juvenile crime is the prime example where figures based on actual offences both overlook the discretion applied by law enforcement agencies and the effects of detection efficiency. As we have already noted in Chapter Four, there is now evidence both that the police charge some children and not others (Cicourel, 1967; Parker et al, 1981), and that the actual rate of offending is much higher than that revealed by official figures (Hindenlang, 1976; West and Farrington, 1973). Clearly, an accurate account of the effects of social policy in the area of juvenile crime could not be undertaken by reference solely to official statistics.

The same is true of the effects of social services' intervention in the lives of families. For many years, until Mayer and Timms published *The Client Speaks* in 1970, it was accepted practice that the effects of social work intervention were assessed by asking social workers to describe their practice and (sometimes) by objective assessment of clients. The concept that social intervention could have effects unintended by the practitioners and which could only be revealed by asking the clients for their *subjective* impressions, took a long time to achieve currency, and had to do battle with the time-honoured attitude in professional practice that the client could not be expected to know what he, or more usually, she wanted. The even more extraordinary notion, that clients' opinions could be used to reshape social work practice into a more effective intervention, and that social policy itself could be responsive to the views of its recipients, has taken even longer to achieve respectability amongst social commentators.

Launched by Mayer and Timms and continued by, among others, Sainsbury and his colleagues at the University of Sheffield, this new approach to the evaluation of social work has revealed previously uncharted areas of knowledge, and has been extensively reviewed in recent years (Sainsbury, 1980; Craig, 1981; Rees and Wallace, 1982; Fisher, 1983). One overriding finding from these reviews is that social work has many effects on its clients of which its practitioners are unaware and which they cannot intend. The potential for misinterpretation and imperfect communication in the interactions between workers and clients is enormous, and no analysis of the effects of social work intervention can be complete without some attention to the views of those on the receiving end.

This dimension to social policy is especially relevant to the question of how public intervention in the lives of families where child care difficulties have arisen can be most effective. As we have seen, for example, the raw fact that an admission to care takes place as a result of a care order made by the court, and thus appears in official statistics as further evidence of compulsion, may tell us little about how this action is experienced by either the child or by his or her family. Our research revealed that a significant number of such admissions were, in fact, perceived by the parents as a direct result of their requesting help, and that in such cases the parents actually welcomed the care order as an attempt to meet the needs of their children. This is not to say that all care orders were welcomed by the families; and there is clearly the possibility that while this intervention was favoured by the parents, it was resented by the children.

Nevertheless, such findings illustrate the dangers of using apparently incontrovertible facts to develop an argument about the changing nature of public intervention in child care. Our evidence points to the need both to be sensitive to the many different recipients of public policy and their potentially different views on its effects, and to the need to understand the meaning, to those on the receiving end, of actions taken in the name of public policy.

A new approach

Our argument is therefore that evidence about the changing nature of family life, about the characteristics of present-day parenting, and about the views of clients, points to a clear need to review both the legal/moral framework governing state intervention in the lives of families and the professional practice of those working in child care.

We accept the view advanced by Parton (1981) that all debate over the proper role of the state in guaranteeing acceptable family life for children centres on judgements of what is acceptable parenting and child behaviour, and that such judgements are essentially influenced by the ideological context. In the end, as Dingwall and his colleagues point out (1983), child care policy amounts to a statement on what constitutes 'the good society'.

We are convinced that the philosophy which was originally intended to predominate in the post-war UK child care legislation – namely that the work of public agencies was to provide supportive services to families, part of which could include admission to care as a means ultimately of preserving family relationships in the long run – has been lost from current practice. This loss is both accidental, in the sense of resulting from neglect and omission, and deliberate, in the sense that current social policy is founded on myths and misinformation about family life which tend to polarize the public and private care of children. In our view, this philosophy of *partnership* with clients, in which the primary caring role of the family is reasserted but effectively *supplemented* by public services, must be reintroduced into national policy and practice. The 'good society' must, in our view, treat those in need of child care services as fellow citizens rather than as 'inadequate' parents or children.

8

Rethinking child care practice

The policy issues described in the previous chapter have their counterpart in day-to-day practice. In Britain professional child care social work could be said to date from 1948 when local government Children's Departments were created. The merits of different models of social work practice have been debated over the ensuing years in courses and in agencies, in research units and in professional associations. The experiences of the families and the workers portrayed in this study have taken place in the context of these debates. Two central features in the arguments have always been the ways in which social services can provide good parenting for children, and equally the ways in which the necessity for this can be avoided by preventive work.

Taking parenting first, the State's ability to act as a caring parent has come under scrutiny in Britain in various public enquiries into the deaths of children in care. The past decade or so has also seen increasing questioning of the State's parenting ability from the permanency movement within social work. This has developed the concept of keeping intervention to the minimum in families, and also the need for decisive action on the child's time scale to provide permanent families as a substitute for natural families in certain situations of breakdown (Morris, 1984). In the USA legislation has been framed around some of these permanency ideas (Sinanoglu, 1984).

Moving to prevention, the field appears far less developed. Tunstill's 1982 bibliography of child care social work highlights the paucity of published material on this topic in Britain, and her recent (1985) small-scale survey of agencies indicates that policy and practice developments are none too prominent either. In the USA the picture is rather different, and there appears to be a relatively recent development of prevention as a topic in its own right (see, for example, Mace, 1983). Also, as we shall see, some important research studies do address the issue although normally not under the prevention banner.

Leaving aside the developments in the child care field there have, of course, been changes in social work practice more generally. From around 1950 onward social work practice has been subject to evaluation and investigation, often on quite a grand scale with group-controlled experiments (for a summary of some of the main projects, many of them in America, see Sheldon, 1984). The practice research conducted before the mid-1970s yielded depressing results as regards the general effectiveness of the dominant methods in use with individuals and families (see the 1978 summary by Wood). The research design of these studies, which normally focused on global questions of effectiveness, unfortunately meant that lessons for practice were often difficult to draw out. However there have been more recent studies (usually of an action research nature and with more limited goals) that have started to highlight the element of effective practice. Reid and Hanrahan (1982) have summarized these studies and they comment that there are 'grounds for optimism'. The studies suggest the following general points. Firstly that practitioners should focus on obtaining clients' commitments to undertake specific problem-solving activities; secondly that what is to be done and what is to be gained from doing it should be laid out clearly; and overall that the client should be engaged as far as possible as a partner in the endeavour.

The practice context for this study therefore consists of debates on and developments in the 'three Ps' of child care: parenting, prevention and partnership. We will look at each of these issues in turn, alongside some of the main findings of the study, and see how they might contribute to the development of child care practice.

SOCIAL SERVICES AS PARENTS

Assessing the quality of social services provision of parenting is clearly a highly complex task. However, there are perhaps two themes that would be generally accepted as fundamental prerequisites of care when provided by an agency. The first is that the unique nature of the child and their siblings, parents and others should receive due recognition in the care given. There is a particular need for a personally tailored service in this field; it may be a routine service in parts but its whole must reflect this child, and this family; not the generality of children and of families. Equally, the inevitable involvement of a number of different staff must not result in a conflicting and fragmented provision of care. Although these aims may be carried out in many ways, the possibility of personal consideration and a collaborative team with shared aims must be present for good practice to be achieved. What light does this study shed on these prerequisites of good parenting from social services?

The service that was provided was experienced by the users as personal in the sense that it was personified by their field social worker, and certain personal qualities such as openness, commitment, and reliability in their workers were valued. There was, however, little involvement of the family in the choice of carers and, with residential care, little or no negotiation about the practical arrangements of care. The agency resource allocation and administrative procedures often made this low level of involvement almost inevitable. Social workers described the lack of control they had over resource allocation, and the way that their contribution to most of the arrangements for providing child care was effectively a notification to others to put a routine procedure into action. Although they felt they had a responsible role, they felt subject to, rather than supported by, agency procedures in carrying it out. They said they found it hard to act as the personal representative of their client in this context, and it is not surprising that the general tendency was for families to be fitted into pre-existing categories or patterns of service that were not greatly adapted from case to case.

Clearly the difficulties in providing an adaptable service are great. But worse problems in the field of the elderly, showing for example highly impersonal patterns of residential care (Godlove et al, 1983), are being tackled with some promising results. For example, the Kent Community Care scheme has given social workers a limited budget to provide tailor-made care schemes for the elderly without the use of residential care (Challis and Davis, 1980). There are examples of respite care fostering for the elderly that show how services can be personally developed (Leat, 1983). While there are current examples of such practices in child care, they are by no means the norm. The problem of devolving control of resources and services to suitably accountable front-line staff needs urgent consideration. Without more development in this direction it is difficult to see how social workers can tailor services, and as long as they face a struggle to do this, their clients will face the possibility of a service they must try to adapt to, rather than one adapted to them.

The second factor that agency parenting is bound to face is the need for different staff members to share common aims and work as a collaborative team. The workers in this study expressed their concern that this was not always the case, and the families maintained that the lack of shared aims could sometimes rebound directly on themselves. These issues were closely linked with the very different experiences of residential staff and foster parents on the one hand, and social workers on the other. People with direct responsibility for day-to-day care of the child found themselves facing many of the same issues concerning behaviour that the parents had attempted to cope with before care. They developed views of the child based upon a degree of contact that had previously only been known by the parents. Although a balance sheet covering a child's good and bad points would probably not be identical with the parents' one, and although their explanations concerning child behaviour would be likely to differ, there was a strong shared experiential link between care staff/foster parents and natural parents. There was usually empathy and often sympathy concerning the particular experience of bringing up this particular child. In the case of foster parents, this was usually reinforced by a moderate degree of knowledge of previous home circumstances arising from information and contact from child, parents and social worker. Residential staff, working on shifts, and responsible for a group of children, often had less likelihood of direct contact and rather slim information from social workers. Their experiences were therefore slightly less closely aligned with natural parents' but they were still significantly different from the field social workers'.

The fieldworkers had regular contact with the child and accepted statutory and agency responsibilities for child care plans. Unlike the parents they were more likely to view care as a break-up in family composition as compared with a variation, albeit a very significant one, in the pattern of parenting in the family. Their experiences thus tended to emphasize the views of the child alone. The agency care-givers, and the social workers, were each therefore likely to put a different complexion on the picture they held of the family as a whole. This difference in perspective could be the subject of discussion and be recognized and constructively used. But there were barriers in the way of both discussion and recognition.

In general, communication between field and residential staff was not very extensive. Information was shared but both groups described circumstances where they had had to act in ignorance of important details that were subsequently revealed to them. The general view held by field staff was of residential care as a 'last resort'. It was likely to minimize a constructive view of residential care, and may have contributed to a rather inactive field role in communicating information. Residential staff felt themselves to be at the bottom of the pile in social services, and suggested that there were occasions when a request for information or a potential contribution to information was simply ignored. To some degree they shared a view of residential care as a last resort. They expressed views on the inadequacy of care which could mirror the parents' views of the family problems that led to care, such as changing care-givers and difficult peers for the children. Foster parents did not share the last resort view, but were unsure of their right to ask for information and could tend towards diffidence in their dealings with social workers. Firm conclusions from our small fostering sample are not possible, but there were indications that foster parents were told more and learnt more than the residential staff. Both foster parents and the care staff jointly recognized one last barrier to communication, which arose from the continuing sense of the major responsibility for a child lying with field staff alone. Descriptions by care-givers of telephone calls to fieldworkers to check, for example, if visits to parents were allowed or if schooling decisions were correct, were tinged with aggravation that this responsibility lay with field staff, and with worry about the boundaries of the care-givers' own powers. All-in-all it made an uneasy context for open communication and the development of a coherent approach to the family's needs.

Proposals to improve communication and collaboration within the child care team must recognize the differences in perspective of the different staff members. It has been a long-standing concern of child care practitioners that minimum numbers of staff should be directly involved with children in care (Parker, 1980). This is clearly consonant with the suggestion highlighted earlier of aiming for the maximum devolution of resources. It should, of course, also have an effect in reducing the communication and collaboration problems. Perhaps the question 'Is it really necessary for you to be currently involved with this case?' should be asked of all members of the care team at regular intervals. Carefully and thoughtfully asked and answered it might have significantly good effects on practice.

There are still going to be major difficulties in communication. Two current practice developments seem pertinent to reducing them. Firstly there is a slow development towards the creation of family centres where field and residential roles are mixed. If experiences can be shared by social workers providing some direct care and some family work in the community, then the inbuilt problems of differing perspectives are reduced. This study would lend support to the development of projects that provide field services from residential units, and that attempt the maximum integration of field, residential and foster parent roles. Secondly there is a growing use of written agreements in social work practice (for a general discussion see Sheldon, 1980). In child care, written agreements may incorporate a common view of clients and workers, or they may make explicit the differences in the views. They can be reviewed, provide indicators of progress, specify tasks and aims and so on. Research has shown them to be positively linked with reduction of permanent family breakdown (Stein et al, 1974), and there are some promising practice developments in fostering (Kent Family Placement Service, 1985) and elsewhere in child care (Hussell, 1983). A Parliamentary report on child care has added its voice to a growing recognition of their importance (House of Commons, 1984). Recent practice models based on effectiveness research, such as task-centred work (Reid, 1978) and behavioural approaches (Gambrill, 1983), have also been instrumental in highlighting the value of explicit, written and shared statements of aims and understandings. In highlighting the real difficulties of providing a personal child care service, our study provides an additional reason for adopting written agreements as one element of practice.

PREVENTION IN CHILD CARE

We have seen in Chapter Seven that child care policy development has tended to assume an antipathy between public care and family care. The reality of family life is, of course, more complex than this. Many families use childminders, summer camps, and boarding schools to provide care for their children. On the other hand, many children in care see their parents, stay with them and other relatives, and so on. The simplistic dichotomy of family care and public care is also seen in the development of child care practice. Prevention and rehabilitation, for example, are often seen as distinct from care itself. Prevention of care precedes care, and rehabilitation home ends it. If public care is taken to be one of the provisions available to help families and children, then the idea of prevention can change to prevention of permanent family breakdown, rather than prevention of care. Care itself could play a part in prevention. It may be a breathing space, it may be a time for parents to learn new skills or children new behaviours, but its focus would be on the continuation of a family, not the removal of a child. Rehabilitation, prevention and care could be understood as a unified practice; we will later suggest that this practice could be termed 'assisted parenting'. Of course it is important to recognize that this may not be possible, and children may need protection from their families. Such families may be legally required to separate, and the child will need permanent care elsewhere. The parents will need help, if they are willing or able to accept it, to make a different sort of life apart from their child. This situation is true for a small minority of cases, but even for these the explicit clarity of view and purpose which appears so important in the rest of child care work can only aid the protection role.

The view of prevention as possibly *including* public care as one part of attempts to avert irretrievable family breakdown appears to be gathering some support (Maluccio, 1984; Tunstill, 1985). This study would add its weight to that and provides particular information on the three important stages that such an approach could involve: family attempts at solving child care problems, contact between children in care and their families, and the work around and after discharge to maintain any gains made while in care.

Problem-solving

The parents in this study arrived at social services (or a court) with family problems that were long-standing, and with their appearance usually being triggered by one particular event which was the last straw for them. They saw the problems in terms of the child's attitudes, particularly those concerning lack of respect for adults, and in terms of breaking rules within the family (e.g. times to be in at night), and breaking rules outside the family (e.g. truancy). Parents quite often suggested that the particular child was a problem child, and that he or she was somehow different from the other children in the family. There were frequently worries about the bad company that the child kept. Many of these views were shared by the children themselves, with hints that any difference between them and their brothers and sisters lay in the treatment they received from their parents. This was especially true if family members had changed, for example with the arrival of step-parents or step-siblings. Social workers, on the other hand, rarely shared the parents' sense of the history of the problems, and they had a different perspective on its components. The discrepancies were often not appreciated by families or by social workers. As the social workers' questions often seemed to be at cross-purposes to the families' worries, it was easy for families to feel that they were worrying too much about their problems and that they were not very adequate parents. This occurred alongside the almost universal parental view of the social workers as pleasant, kind, and generally reasonable people (despite many views of the social services department itself as something of a desperate last resort). Because the history of the problems was fairly infrequently held in common, it was possible for social workers to give advice about children that in itself was perfectly sensible, but which actually repeated advice they had already had, and suggested activities they had already tried. At times this was reported by parents as increasing their sense of personal inadequacy.

Parents and children had often made up their minds that care was a suitable solution to their problems, and they described emphasizing this heavily in their discussions with the social worker. This pressure was clearly felt by the social workers, and they usually attempted to resist it, often seeing admission to care as signalling their own inadequacy in providing alternatives to care. By the time care began it was therefore easy for parents to feel their failures had been confirmed, and for social workers to feel their intervention was also relatively unsuccessful.

The experiences of clients and workers at the point of entry into care could be a most unfortunate beginning for any attempt at problem-solving. Both groups felt that the outcome highlighted their weaknesses. The focus on failure to solve problems could leave a vacuum of solutions which was only filled by care itself. Care was therefore likely to be the only answer rather than part of an answer. From the parents' and children's points of view, care was therefore a moderately positive step in a history of family failure. Workers and clients generally saw very few indications of family strengths that would now *support* the care solution. The provision of care was usually seen as a package to be delivered, rather than a participative initiative in sharing or changing parenting. For the social workers it was often the end of an intervention of theirs which had focused on preventing care. It was the beginning of a new phase concerned with managing the rather unsatisfactory business of care itself.

Social workers often therefore perceived entry to care as a failure of practice. Our study did not examine the appropriateness of care. Nonetheless the research team did not think that any admissions were notably inappropriate, and the circumstances of families often appeared desperate, with little realistic option to some period of care (sometimes, of course, the courts also gave no option). It is important to note that studies that have looked at decision-making (e.g. Packman et al, 1984) have failed to find major differences between families that do gain entry to care and those where it is seriously considered but refused. These latter families also contain a group that is notably resentful of the lack of help, as they see it, from social workers with their family problems.

It seems inevitable, and reasonable, that many requests for some form of care will be agreed. The practice dilemma concerns the ways in which such agreement can then be developed as part of a joint approach to family problems between worker and client. Problem-exploration clearly needs to be wide-ranging, and an accompanying reinforcement of strengths is needed. All of this sounds an onerous and skilled task, and indeed it is. But it does indicate where we should be looking for the practice models to develop in preventive child care. For example, task-centred social work provides a model of problem-exploration and develops a partnership approach to practice that is likely to be very relevant to preventive approaches in child care (Reid, 1978 and 1981; Epstein, 1980 and 1982; Goldberg et al, 1985). The task-centred approach is characterized by an emphasis on joint problem-solving activity that is agreed between workers and clients, and is an active planned intervention. In America action research projects have successfully developed families' abilities to cope, and have reduced the long-term care population (Stein and Gambrill, 1977). The models of practice used have drawn on learning theory and again have been active planned intervention undertaken in close collaboration with the client. These also look promising developments for the future. Finally there have been changes made and evaluated in the provision of services so that child care support can be obtained quickly and can be tailored to individual family needs (Burt and Balyeat, 1977). The services have included 24 hour access to home-makers who can join a family for brief periods, and providing services that are quickly accessible after court hearings; the emphasis is on accessibility to a service that can be quickly tailored to personal needs. All of these projects have initial implementation costs but none have consumed extra resources in the longer term. There are, then, significant difficulties for the business of problem-solving with child care cases, but there are equally helpful signs that answers are being developed within social work practice in general and American child care research in particular.

Parental involvement in care

The decision about the first placement of the child in care may set a pattern of parental involvement which is maintained throughout care. The placement decision was usually seen by the social workers, and experienced by the families, as a professional and administrative one that was not subject to much family influence. There was some indication that this was slightly less true for fostering as compared with residential placements. As we have already mentioned, the social workers who made a point of involving families as far as they could still found themselves subject to agency allocation procedures which were generally routinized rather than tailored to the individual, and which involved a sequence of internal meetings and processes that left agency voices greatly outweighing the clients'. Clients usually had no opportunity to object to this as they had little idea of the discussions behind the scenes, and they anyway assumed that professional allocation was the norm. That they would have a continuing involvement beyond allocation was simply taken for granted by them.

The problems they experienced with involvement once care was established were partly practical ones of travel and available time for visits, and partly social difficulties of the visiting process and of the feeling that they were taking more responsibility for maintaining involvement than they had expected, and indeed than they thought was right. The social and practical difficulties of visiting absent family members are clearly evident in many circumstances in life, for example visiting friends in hospital. The circumstances were compounded here not only by the fraught nature of the reason for absence but also by the uncertainty, as the parents saw it, about who they should see in a children's home, and the difficulties of feeling part of a group that had changing members and, for many parents, unsatisfactory rules and norms. So, for residential care at least, parents said they were often faced with staff who were new to them and appeared to have little knowledge of their child. They also had to deal with an atmosphere of relative discord and rowdiness that had parallels with family activity, but was also related to group processes that were novel; concerning, for example, privacy of meetings, use of communal rooms and the children's attitudes to the staff. Residential staff appreciated many of these problems but felt so involved in the practical day-to-day work of providing necessities, maintaining order and generating activities for the young people that there was little energy available to put into easing access. Fostering placements suffered all these difficulties of involvement, with the important exception of the fact that parents had a much clearer idea as to who was in charge, and a somewhat clearer picture of the style of care that their children were receiving.

For children the period of care must inevitably be one of new rules and norms, and of new people and places. They rarely described any particular expectations that they should visit their parental home. The social worker was seen as responsible for this aspect of their lives, although the arranging of visits was done by foster parents/care staff. Ambiguity and confusion about parental involvement was relatively common. Many of the contacts with people and places associated with their home had, of course, ended with care, and for some children complete changes of friendship and their use of evenings and weekend could occur.

Although both parents and children felt that there was a continuing and major link between them, the practical enactment of that link was not straightforward. Without active work on it the regular contact and shared activity which are such important parts of a feeling of belonging could easily diminish. It was the exception and not the rule for social workers to initiate such active work, and for residential staff/foster parents to maintain it.

Links between parents and children may be diminished unncessarily by care. Others have explored this particular issue of family links in some depth (Millham et al, 1984 and 1985). From the point of view of prevention and rehabilitation, the lack of attention to such links and the difficulties experienced in maintaining them are particularly important. The study by Jones and his colleagues (1976) in America suggested that an active focus on family involvement paid significant returns in the numbers of children who went home. Active plans for the involvement of parents, outside of the very small minority of abuse and protection cases, are likely to be an important element of better child care. These plans and the relevant actions to carry them out call for the development of practice in an area which is, as yet, little explored. There is much to guide us in managing separation, and there is also material in helping children and families unite, but there is a notable gap between these two phases. The creation of a preventive framework for care would benefit by developments in practice and research in this area.

Work towards discharge

If the provision of care is going to be a constructive part of the solution to a family's problems, and if it is going to be focused on the prevention of permanent family breakdown, then discharge from care must be an important ingredient of the overall provisions of help. It may occur quickly, or in stages, or only after quite lengthy periods of care, but it will be, for the vast majority of children, part of the desired outcome. It will need to be an issue under active review, as indeed English law requires for children in voluntary care where the social services shall 'in all cases where it appears to them consistent with the welfare of the child to do so, endeavour to ensure that the care of the child is taken over either by a parent or guardian, or . . . relative . . .' (Child Care

Act 1980, S.2(3)). The great majority of children in voluntary care do indeed return to their parents and for most of them care is quite short, often under eight weeks. If the service for this group or for the offenders and others who are in care compulsorily is to be a fully rehabilitative one, then discharges should follow work aimed at overcoming obstacles to parental care. They should be accompanied by work which seeks to maintain home or child changes after care itself. That is to say that discharges should be linked to the purpose of care, and form part of an active plan that provides appropriate help in maintaining new strengths after formal care ends.

In practice we have seen that discharge from care was usually perceived by both families and staff as resulting from pressure from the family, rather than as a consequence of planned worker and family actions. In admission the worker played a central role, in discharge the family usually took the lead. Indeed some children, for example, simply relocated themselves at home and left it to foster parents or care staff to inform social workers. Only the discharge of court care orders actively involved the social worker. But it was not, in the families' view, usually closely linked to solving problems or maintaining change. It typically took place after a period of being returned home (still the subject of a court order) that seemed to families to be a test period of indeterminate length. All had agreed that one of the purposes of care was to stop the young person offending. By the time these young people had gone home all were also agreed that if no offences occurred while at home then the court order should be discharged. However the necessary length of this period was often not clear to families, nor was it clear to them what help, if they needed it, they would receive during it.

Nearly all the discharges took place as an individual transaction between worker and family (although in court cases a senior social worker was involved for legal and other advice). There was hardly any mention of the co-operation of care staff or foster parents in active work over discharge, nor was there mention of schools and other youth services being involved. Any work that was designed to maintain changes achieved by care was seen as limited to worker and family, and not as involving other individuals, agencies or networks in the families' lives. Much as care tended to be seen as a self-contained solution, rather than as part of a solution, so discharge home tended to the same self-contained perspective. If care was ended, it was likely that other work with the family would cease.

When considering the other aspects of prevention and rehabilitation earlier we suggested that clarity over the problems to be solved, active techniques to tackle them and to build on strengths, and skills of managing links were all important elements of an improved child care practice. Clearly all of these elements also have a role to play in making discharge a constructive outcome. They are likely to help the families with the discharge process and its aftermath. Our study examined only those cases where discharge was definitely going to occur, and so we do not know if there are situations where families might be helped towards discharge by the use of different models of practice such as we have suggested earlier. In the American studies there are strong suggestions that this might be the case. For example, Emlen and his colleagues (1978) developed an action research project using carefully structured reviews of approximately 500 children who had been in care for over one year and who were identified as unlikely to return home. Despite this identification, around one-quarter of the children did, in fact, return home following the active intervention of the project workers. Their model of practice, directed at first towards providing permanent placements at home, and subsequently towards permanent placement via adoption, would fit the promising approaches mentioned earlier. So discharge problems add to the pressure to rethink child care practice along the lines of a new agreement based on a purposive model. Such a model would inevitably include a focus on the various networks that are important in the construction and solution of family child care problems. The active involvement, for example, of relevant relatives, and of relevant agencies, such as schools, would be regularly sought. Discharge of court order cases highlights one particular group within these networks, that of the judiciary. If purposive agreements are to be made with families, and if court discharge is to feature within them, there are professional, legal, and indeed practical reasons for engaging in an active dialogue with the judiciary about the nature and purpose of social work practice. Probation Officers have long held regular judicial meetings concerned with their work in the courts, and the provision of alternatives to custody. Social workers have been less forward in this respect, but judicial and social work practice are often closely linked in child care and a closer dialogue is now due.

The boundaries of care

At entry to care clients and workers often see care as a solution in its own right. Once care has begun it can operate in ways which tend not to encourage the maintenance of parental involvement. Then the ending of care is rarely part of an active plan, and the maintenance of gains made during care may go by default. In summary, these problems for the preventive and rehabilitative ideals all concern the boundaries of care. From a professional point of view care is something that is given or withheld, and it is quite distinct from the general patterns of parenting that occur in family life. If this is to change, then a new orientation towards care as a service, and towards care as one possible part of preventing permanent family breakdown, needs to be accompanied by the use of skills and knowledge such as those from the various practice models and research projects that have been mentioned. Training and research are likely to be increasingly called upon in future years. But agency changes are necessary for the development of this preventive framework, as it would require a significant shift towards an emphasis on professional development rather than procedural control, and towards social worker control of resources rather than central allocation. The most fundamental argument within all of these changes may be the need for a change in the professional view taken of clients. The client is the central concern of the agency, and the ways in which this concern can be conceptualized form the last stage of this reformulation of child care practice.

CLIENTS OR PARTNERS?

It was argued in Chapter Seven that there are good grounds for reintroducing a philosophy of partnership into the public child care services. This would entail a general orientation of services towards providing supportive help for families, including if necessary the use of care, as a means of ultimately preserving family relationships. In the vast majority of circumstances it would lead to the reuniting of family members, in some circumstances it would preserve memories and contacts in continued separation, and in a tiny minority it would lead to permanent placements with little contact with natural family but where psychological links with the families of origin were suitably sustained (e.g. life-story books for children). The notion of a partnership that could lead to these different results does not differ markedly from ideas of partnership in other areas of life. There are probably few, if any, examples of partnership where it would be reasonably suggested that the partners are entirely equal in all respects, and there are probably no genuine partnerships that continue to exist without all the partners being prepared to work hard at the maintenance of partnership itself. To view a client as a partner is not therefore simply to view a client as a user. In child care social work in particular such a view would quickly founder on the important role of social workers in the protection of children.

Partnership is more akin to a philosophy of practice which could inform all the actions undertaken by social workers, so that clients could reasonably ask for an account to be given, and expect their views to carry weight in connection with the child care processes they are experiencing. For the social worker an accurate account of their work should anyway be necessary within the agency, and at times within the courts. What would be necessary for child care practice to offer an account to clients and to give due recognition to their views?

Accountability

The degree of direct responsibility that clients have for determining the social work actions undertaken with them varies widely according to many factors. Young children as compared with teenage children, for example, should participate differently in plans for their own future. Equally, parents using a voluntary service and those whose children are subject to court orders should have different levels of formal involvement. But there is formal involvement and there is the feeling of involvement and the two, as we have seen, are potentially quite different matters. The common factor, if a partnership approach is to be adopted, is that participants should be able to call for an account of what is going on, with whom, and with what aims. They should feel they have a right to this account. How it is phrased (e.g. for junior school children) and what action families or workers can take to change it (e.g. the constraints of a court order) are subsidiary matters to the primary stage of receiving an account. The amount of detail to be expected in an account should presumably be enough for a person without specialized knowledge to be able to understand what actions are due to occur over the relevant time period, and what observable changes would indicate the success or failure of the work.

No one who has read the study in the preceding chapters will be under any illusion about the difficulties of providing a proper account in the complex and often fraught circumstances of family problems, and in a large social services agency. But it is equally the case that models of practice based upon explicit and jointly shared information about problems, aims, and desired outcomes (i.e. potential accounts) have been used in settings and circumstances that cover the entire range of child care work.

As noted earlier, key American examples are summarized in Lindsay (1982), and some of the British examples are in Morris (1984). The notion of contract and account is central to a number of practice projects (Hussell, 1983; Kent Family Placement Scheme, 1985). Practice developments mentioned earlier, such as behavioural contracting and task-centred models, are fully consonant with an accountable approach. They emphasize the importance of an attempt to seek clarity and understanding (although, of course, not always agreements) between social workers and clients. These are the approaches that look very hopeful for the development of a partnership in child care. They do, however, call for social workers to have both the necessary skills and the necessary authority. As we have noted earlier, training programmes and agency policies are both needed. An account must be given in a clear way but it must also be given by the person with authority to enact its elements. In a personal service, demanding quick responses, the social worker is the focus for both client and agency when accounts are called for. The clear location of responsibility on the social worker has ramifications for agencies that will need considerable thought and possibly far-reaching changes. Social workers feel responsible at present, as our study has shown, but formal responsibility can often lie with residential placement allocation groups, team managers, or even at senior management level. Lines of responsibility within agencies may need careful review if a genuine account, directly given to the clients themselves, is to be a key part of practice.

Recognition of views

We have discussed elsewhere the complicated role of client views in good social work practice (Fisher, 1983). In child care, differing professional and client views may at times require resolution in a court, and they will often be the subject of detailed negotiation. But there is a primary stage of partnership practice. A clear recognition of all the participants' views must underpin any of the subsequent debates concerning what is to be done. This study has shown the difficult task that social workers face in their attempts to understand clients' views. Family views are often rooted in long-standing and complex issues, they can differ markedly between family members, they can be difficult to obtain if, for example, emotions are high or if adolescent sulkiness is being prominently displayed. It is often quite remarkable how accurate social workers can be about their clients' views considering the unpropitious circumstances in which they may be conveyed. But there are gaps. Different family members tend to be neglected at different times (e.g. children before entry to care, fathers after entry to care). Agreement regarding the use of concepts can be incorrectly taken for granted rather than tested (e.g. the meaning to parents of the changes in rights that occur when children enter care). These basic issues could be diminished if clients made a forceful approach to their social workers, saying such things as 'I'd be grateful for my views to play a role here' and 'Would you mind repeating back to me what I've just said so I could check you've understood it'. This tongue-in-cheek suggestion highlights the responsibility that social workers have to make the client role less difficult. If views are to be properly recognized they must be elicited and checked in ways that accommodate the clients' circumstances and needs. Once again the practice models mentioned earlier are relevant and a range of techniques within behavioural contact and task-centred models seems likely to play an important part in establishing a basic recognition of views.

The next stage

In Chapter Seven we argued that child care policy could and should develop with an underlying philosophy of partnership between the State and families. In this chapter we have examined some of the practice implications of such a development and put them alongside the experiences of families and workers found by our study. The welfare of the child is the essential component of the policy and practice under discussion here. The provision of parenting to safeguard that welfare is seen as a dual responsibility of state and family, with no easy answers about where the boundaries should be drawn on different occasions and in different circumstances. The majority of families will find parenting an onerous but rewarding task, and a minority will find themselves unable to cope. These families will seek help from social services, and a few may find themselves subject to supervision and control. The experience for the children is perhaps best expressed as one of 'assisted parenting', of receiving parenting over and above their own families' efforts. This assisted parenting may involve brief respite care away from home, and for a minority of children it may involve permanent care away from their families. To view it as assisted parenting allows for the spectrum of assistance that is available, and maintains a focus on the welfare of the child. The partnership between the State and the family that is enacted for all children (whether being born or graduating) is thrown into sharp relief for families requesting or receiving assisted parenting. The provision of this is surely one of the most difficult tasks that our society asks of any of its agencies.

The study we have reported here was designed to explore the experiences of families and workers engaged in these difficult situations. The experiences have, we hope, been faithfully conveyed, and they will enter the continuing debate about the best way to encourage and safeguard the welfare of children. The next stage is the most important one. Child care policy and practice emphasizing partnership and assisted parenting can be seen in fragmented form in parts of legislation, some agencies and a number of practice developments. Pulling these elements together will be a programme for a decade.

A note for the American reader

There is a long history of the constructive interchange of ideas between social workers in the United Kingdom and in the United States of America, and the study and conclusions reported here will have wide relevance in the American system. Care has been taken to try to use terms which are not specific to one country's form of organization and legislation, but for the American reader who has had little contact with the UK a very brief note is given below about the framework of public child care practice in England and Wales (there are differences in Scotland and Northern Ireland).

Children's services are in general provided by the local tier of government serving a county or district. Schools and social services are both the general responsibility of this tier. Residential care, substitute family care (called fostering in the UK), most of the work in the (juvenile) courts and general advice and help about social problems are all provided by these public social services. Income maintenance is not their role and is provided by a national department. There are some large private charities for children but much of their work is now developmental.

The local social services operate in a framework of legislation laid down by central government (the Department of Health and Social Security) in Parliament. Social services *may* provide care outside the home under this legislation, and *must* provide it if courts determine that they should do so because of the need to protect a child, or because a child has committed a crime and is seen as in need of help. When we consider the implications of the study (Chapters Seven and Eight), reference is made to the overall general duty contained in legislation that social services should seek to prevent the need for care away from the home, and that children should go home from care whenever desirable and possible. Reference is also made to 'voluntary care' where care away from home has been directly requested by parents, and to a child on a 'care order' or 'remanded in care', or subject to a place of safety when care has been ordered by a court. The main legislation for 'voluntary care' is the Child Care Act 1980 and for 'care orders', the Children and Young Persons Act 1969. The terms in common use in the legislation and in the practice of care are specifically mentioned at the start of Chapter Two.

Social workers working in the community usually have two years training, and there is a mix of graduates and non-graduates. The training covers all client groups, but there is often some degree of specialization after a few years of practice, with workers selecting an area of work as their predominant interest, or applying for specialized jobs (e.g. in adoption). There is little advanced training available. Many of the workers in the residential units have received very little formal training.

Legislation, policy, and professional practice in Britain and America are, of course, different in numerous ways. The American reader of this study will detect the differences at various times, but will recognize over and above this the common problems and debates that are of pressing concern on both sides of the Atlantic in the development of child care services.

References

ALCOCK, A., and HARRIS, P., *Welfare Law and Order*, Macmillan, 1982.

BERRIDGE, D., *Children's Homes*, Blackwell, 1985.

BERRY, J., *Daily Experiences in Residential Life: a Study of Children and Their Care-givers*, Routledge and Kegan Paul, 1975.

BLAXTER, M., and PATTERSON, E., *Mothers and Daughters*, Heinemann Education, 1982.

BURGOYNE, J., and CLARK, D., 'Reconstituted Families' in RAPOPORT et al, eds., *Families in Britain*, Routledge and Kegan Paul, 1982, pp. 286–302.

BURT, M.R., and BALYEAT, R.R., *A Comprehensive Emergency Service for Neglected and Abused Children*, Vantage Press, New York, 1977.

CHALLIS, D., and DAVIES, B., 'A New Approach to Community Care for the Elderly', in *British Journal of Social Work*, vol. 10, no. 1, 1980, pp. 1–18.

CICOUREL, A., *The Social Organisation of Juvenile Justice*, John Wiley, New York, 1967.

COFFIELD, F., ROBINSON, J., and SARSBY, J., *A Cycle of Deprivation? A Case Study of Four Families*, Heinemann Education, 1982.

CRAIG, G., *Review of Studies of the Public and Users' Attitudes Opinions and Expressed Needs with Respect to Social Work and Social Workers*, National Institute for Social Work, 1981.

DAVIS, A., *The Residential Solution*, Tavistock, 1981.

DINGWALL, R., and EEKELAAR, J., *Care Proceedings*, Blackwell, 1982.

DINGWALL, R., EEKELAAR, J., and MURRAY, T., *The Protection of Children: State Intervention in Family Life*, Blackwell, 1983.

EMLEN, A., LAHTI, J., DOWNS, G., MCKAY, A., and DOWNS, S., *Overcoming Barriers to Planning for Children in Care*, US Children's Bureau, Dept of Health, Education and Welfare, Washington, DC, 1978.

EPSTEIN, L., *Helping People: the Task-Centred Approach*, C.V. Mosby & Co., St Louis, Missouri, 1980.

EPSTEIN, L., *How to Provide Social Services with Task-Centred Methods*, British adaptation by Anne Vickery, National Institute for Social Work, 1982.

FINER REPORT, *Report of the Committee on One-Parent Families*, HMSO, 1974.

FISHER, M., NEWTON, C., and SAINSBURY, E., *Mental Health Social Work Observed*, George Allen and Unwin, 1984.

FISHER, M., ed., *Speaking of Clients*, Joint Unit for Social Services Research, University of Sheffield, 1983.

GAMBRILL, E., *Casework: a Competency Based Approach*, Prentice-Hall, Englewood Cliffs, New Jersey, 1983.

GILLER, H., and MORRIS, A., *Care and Discretion*, Burnet Books, 1981.

GODLOVE, C., RICHARD, L., and RODWELL, G. *Time for Action*, Joint Unit for Social Services Research, University of Sheffield, 1982.

GOLDBERG, E.M., GIBBONS, J., and SINCLAIR, I. *Problems, Tasks and Outcomes*, Allen and Unwin, 1985.

HINDENLANG, M., 'With a Little Help from Their Friends: Group Participation in Reported Delinquent Behaviour', in the *British Journal of Criminology*, no. 16, 1976, pp. 109–25.

HOGGET, B., *Parents and Children*, Sweet and Maxwell, 1981.

HOUSE OF COMMONS, *The Second Report from the Social Services Committee – Session 1983–84 – Children in Care*, HMSO, 1984.

HUSSELL, C., 'Understanding Contracts', in *Adoption and Fostering*, vol. 7, no. 3, 1983, pp. 22–4.

JONES, M.A., NEUMAN, R., and SHYNE, A.W., *A Second Chance for Families – Evaluation of a Program to Reduce Foster Care*, Child Welfare League of America, New York, 1976.

KENT FAMILY PLACEMENT SERVICE, *Ten Years On – a Pioneer Teenage Fostering Scheme*, Kent County Council Social Services Department, 1985.

KOSA, J., ed., *Poverty and Health: a Sociological Analysis*, Harvard University Press, Cambridge, Mass., 1975.

LAMB, M., ed., *The Role of the Father in Child Development*, John Wiley, New York, 1981.

LEAT, D., *A Home from Home*, Research Perspectives on Ageing no. 7, Age Concern, 1983.

LEWIS, G.H., and LEWIS, J.F., 'The Dog in the Night-time: Negative Evidence in Social Research', *British Journal of Sociology*, vol. 31, 1980, pp. 544–58.

LINDSAY, D., 'Achievements for Children in Foster Care', in *Social Work*, vol. 27, 1982, pp. 491–8.

LONGFIELD, J., *Ask the Family*, Bedford Square Press, 1984.

MCKINLEY, K., 'Some Approaches and Problems in the Study of the Use of Services – an Overview', in the *Journal of Health and Social Behaviour*, no. 13, 1972, pp. 115–52.

MACE, D., ed., *Prevention in Family Services*, Sage, Beverley Hills,

California, 1983.

MALUCCIO, A.N., 'Permanency Planning: Implications for Practice with Natural Parents', in *Adoption and Fostering*, vol. 8, no. 4, 1984, pp. 15–20.

MAYER, J.E., and TIMMS, N., *The Client Speaks*, Routledge and Kegan Paul, 1970.

MILLHAM, S., BULLOCK, R., HOSIE, K., and HAAK, M., 'The Problem of Maintaining Links Between Children in Care and Their Families – a Study of the Child Care Process', in *Report to DHSS*, 1984.

MILLHAM, S., BULLOCK, R., HOSIE, K., and LITTLE, M., 'Maintaining Family Links of Children in Care', in *Adoption and Fostering*, vol. 9, no. 2, 1985, pp. 12–16.

MORONEY, R., *The Family and the State*, Longman, 1976.

MORRIS, C., *The Permanency Principle in Child Care Planning*, University of East Anglia, 1984.

MORRIS, A., GILLER, H., SZWED, E., and GEACH, H., *Justice for Children*, Macmillan, 1980.

MORRIS, P., COOPER, J., and BYLES, A., 'Public Attitudes to Problem Solving', in the *British Journal of Social Work*, vol. 3, 1973, pp. 301–20.

MULLEN, E.J., 'The Construction of Personal Models for Effective Practice: a Method for Utilising Research Findings to Guide Social Intervention', in the *Journal of Social Service Research*, vol. 2, 1978, pp. 45–63.

MULLEN, E.J., 'Personal Practice Models', in ROSENBLATT, A., and WALDFOGEL, D., eds., *Handbook of Clinical Social Work*, Jossey Bass, 1983, pp. 623–49.

OAKLEY, A., *The Sociology of Housework*, Martin Robertson, 1974.

OAKLEY, A., *Subject Women*, Martin Robertson, 1981.

PACKMAN, J., *The Child's Generation*, 2nd edition, Blackwell, 1981.

PAGE, R., and CLARK, S., *Who Cares? Young People in Care Speak Out*, National Children's Bureau, 1977.

PARKER, H., CASBURN, M., and TURNBULL, D., *Receiving Juvenile Justice*, Blackwell, 1981.

PARKER, R., 'Foster care in context', in *Adoption and Fostering*, vol. 93, no. 3, 1978, pp. 27–32.

PARKER, R., *Caring for Separated Children: Plans, Procedures, Priorities*, Macmillan, 1980.

PARTON, N., 'The Natural History of Child Abuse: a Study in Social Problem Definition', in the *British Journal of Social Work*, vol. 9, no. 4, 1979, pp. 431–51.

PARTON, N., 'Child Abuse, Social Anxiety and Welfare', *British Journal of Social Work*, vol. 11, no. 4, 1981, pp. 391–414.

PHILLIPS, D., 'Mayer and Timms Revisited: the Evaluation of Client Studies' in FISHER, M., ed., *Speaking of Clients*, Joint Unit for Social Services Research, University of Sheffield, 1983, pp. 8–23.

PHILLIPS, D., and MARSH, P., 'Doing Social Work Research', *Research, Policy and Planning*, vol. 2, no. 2, 1984, pp. 21–7.

RAPOPORT, R., RAPOPORT, R.N., STRELITZ, Z., and KEW, S., *Fathers, Mothers and Others*, Routledge and Kegan Paul, 1977.

RAPOPORT, R., FOGARTY, M., and RAPOPORT, R.N., eds., *Families in Britain*, Routledge and Kegan Paul, 1982.

REES, S., and WALLACE, A., *Verdicts on Social Work*, Arnold, 1982.

REID, W.J., *The Task-Centred System*, Columbia University Press, New York, 1978.

REID, W.J., 'Family Treatment Within a Task-Centred Framework' in TOLSON, E.R., and REID, W.J., eds., *Models of Family Treatment*, Columbia University Press, New York, 1981, pp. 306–31.

REID, W.J., and HANRAHAN, P., 'Recent Evaluations of Social Work: Grounds for Optimism', *Social Work*, vol. 27, 1982, pp. 328–40.

ROWE, J., CAIN, H., HUNDLEBY, M., and KEANE, H., *Long-term Foster Care*, Batsford, 1984.

SAINSBURY, E., 'Research into Client Opinion', in *Social Work Today*, vol. 11, no. 37, 1980, pp. 16–19.

SAINSBURY, E.E., NIXON, S., and PHILLIPS, D., *Social Work in Focus*, Routledge and Kegan Paul, 1982.

SCHWARTZ, H., and JACOBS, J., *Qualitative Sociology – A Method to the Madness*, Free Press, New York, 1979.

SHELDON, B., *The Use of Contracts in Social Work*, British Association of Social Workers, 1980.

SHELDON, B., 'Group-Controlled Experiments in the Evaluation of Social Work Services' in LISHMAN, J., ed., *Research Highlights No. 8 – Evaluation*, Kogan Page, 1984, pp. 97–122.

SINANOGLU, P.A., 'From Drift to Permanency: The US 1980 Legislation', in *Adoption and Fostering*, vol. 8, no. 4, 1984, pp. 10–14.

STEIN, T.J., and GAMBRILL, E.D., 'Facilitating Decision Making in Foster Care', *Social Service Review*, vol. 51, 1977, pp. 502–13.

STEIN, T.J., GAMBRILL, E.D., and WILTSE, K., 'Foster Care: the Use of Contracts', in *Public Welfare*, vol. 32, no. 4, pp. 20–5.

STIMSON, G., and WEBB, B., *Going to See the Doctor*, Routledge and Kegan Paul, 1975.

STREATHER, J., and WEIR, S., *Social Insecurity – Single Mothers on*

Benefit, in *Poverty Pamphlet no. 16*, Child Poverty Action Group, 1974.

TUNSTILL, J., *Social Work with Children – a Bibliography*, University of Surrey, 1982.

TUNSTILL, J., 'Aiming to Prevent Misunderstanding', in *Social Work Today*, vol. 16, no. 40, 1985, pp. 15–17.

WEST, D., and FARRINGTON, D., *Who Becomes Delinquent?*, Heinemann, 1973.

WEST, P., 'Public Preferences for the Care of Dependency Groups', in *Social Science and Medicine*, vol. 18, no. 4, 1984, pp. 287–95.

WILSON, E., *Women and The Welfare State*, Tavistock, 1977.

WILSON, H., 'Parenting in Poverty', *British Journal of Social Work*, vol. 4, no. 3, 1973, pp. 241–54.

WOOD, K.M., 'Casework Effectiveness, a New Look at the Research Evidence', in *Social Work*, vol. 23, 1978, pp. 437–59.

151